The Poetry of
Keats

The Poetry of
Keats
Language &
Experience

David Pollard

THE HARVESTER PRESS • SUSSEX

BARNES & NOBLE BOOKS • NEW JERSEY

First published in Great Britain in 1984 by
THE HARVESTER PRESS LIMITED
Publisher: John Spiers
16 Ship Street, Brighton, Sussex

and in the USA by
BARNES & NOBLE BOOKS
81, Adams Drive, Totowa, New Jersey 07512

© David Pollard, 1984

British Library Cataloguing in Publication Data

Pollard, David.
   The poetry of Keats.
   1. Keats, John, *1795–1821*—Criticism and
   interpretation
   I. Title
   821'.7   PR4837
   ISBN 0–7108–0976–X

Library of Congress Cataloging in Publication Data

Pollard, David.
   The poetry of Keats.

   1. Keats, John, 1795–1821—Criticism and interpretation.
   2. Keats, John, 1795–1821—Philosophy.   I. Title.
   PR4837.P6 1984   821'.7   1984   84–6435
   ISBN 0–389–20490–0

Typeset in Times 10/11 point by Witwell Limited, Liverpool
Printed in Great Britain by Whitstable Litho Ltd, Whitstable, Kent

To my Mother and in memory of my Father

Contents

Preface

On 5 May 1816 John Keats opened the *Examiner* and saw that his first poem had been published. A year before his death he suffered the haemorrhage which he recognised as his 'death warrant' and after which he wrote scarcely any poetry. In the four years between these events he became one of the greatest of English poets.

This is the simple statement of something almost miraculous, and the task of someone with the temerity to approach Keats critically, is to face this miracle. Our interest in Keats the man is provoked by his poetry, and any systematic approach at biography is carried through only in the hope of a return to the poems.

Keats' life is his poetry; or Keats' poetry is his life. The poetry remains the only possible excuse for biography. Divorced from his work Keats would be no more a subject for biography than any other man. Thus the subject of these essays is not Keats but Keats' poetry and the development of his poetic life of which they are the evidence. Indeed, as soon as we embark on such a project we discover that there is very little biography outside of the poetry. Keats himself is silent about the first eighteen years of his life. There remains hardly a single word of his own about his childhood or about the time he spent walking the wards of Guy's Hospital. Attempts to reconstruct this opening two-thirds of Keats' life from second-hand evidence are always more or less guess-work. The real Keats is absent.

Keats remains his own best evidence. When he starts to write, he springs to life complete. His poems and letters are all of a piece: there is no evidence in his letters which helps us to 'understand' the poems, any more than the poems help us to understand the man. His letters are often poetic and his poems often letters. Thus, when Keats writes, he is writing about writing, and this is the only evidence available. Before he is ready to write, there is no evidence. This is what makes him a writer rather than a man who happened also to write. He *is* his writing. At his best he is not writing about anything, least of all about writing; he simply writes.

Likewise, any possible explanation of the best poems subsumes itself in the poetry. But there are times, both in the poems and the letters, when he tries to explain, and it is here, in his Miltonic or conscious writing, that we may try to seek clues.

Our aim is not to superimpose a critical method onto the poetry but to let Keats think poetically—to allow Keats' poetry to bring itself to thought. The poet is a key figure because he offers us the opportunity of undergoing an experience with language, an experience which we usually overlook but which is one of the fundamental experiences of human existence. We are thrown into the flow of language at birth and, for the most part, are at home in it and speak it fluently. But this very fluency depends upon the main attribute of language: the capacity to hide behind that which it speaks about. We live in the flow of language, which grants itself to us without drawing itself to our attention, without allowing us to experience it as it itself is. The best way to explore this seeming paradox is by examining the poets themselves, first because they, above all, possess a privileged relationship with language, and secondly, and more significantly, because it is they who give utterance to that relationship. The poet is of value because he draws us into an experience with language. Verse compositions that fail to do so are not poetry, and prose that does so is poetic.

The aim of these essays is to allow Keats' poetry to speak. Keats was chosen as one of the English poets who gives utterance to this relationship with language, and yet the result is, for the most part, uniquely his. What, hopefully, is here expressed is the act and result of a return to the source of criticism; that is, a return to the text itself. Insofar as these essays say anything which might be related to poetry in general is only to stress this return.

The presiding genius throughout these essays is Martin Heidegger. The idea for them sprang from his later work on the German poets Hölderlin, Rilke, Mörike etc., which of course was written in German. On the whole, English critics have shied away from any attempt to follow up Heidegger's project. There has been little similar work in English on English poets; hence the present attempt.

This is not biography in the usual sense of the term, nor does it attempt an exhaustive journey through Keats' output. Except in its general outline, it is not even chronological. It tends to concentrate on key passages in the hope of drawing the reader into what is poetic in the language itself. Thus some entire poems are excluded, while others are dealt with at greater length than any biographical importance justifies, the aim being to let the poetry speak for itself. The poetry is the pretext for these essays, and the hope is that the reader will be drawn into the poetry on his passage through these essays and that the essays will lose themselves in the text which was their pretext. Insofar as they do this they will have served their purpose.

These essays are therefore exemplary in both senses of the word—as a model of the withdrawal of critique in the face of the text and, consequently, also as a deterrent. Their aim is to make themselves superfluous, to renounce themselves in favour of the text which set them on their way. This is not so say that they are of no use. Their aim is a return to an experience of the poems, not to replace that experience. The hope is that they will prove superfluous but not useless.

Acknowledgements

It would be impossible to name everyone who, in one way or another, over the years, has helped me to clarify my thoughts on Keats. I must, however, put on record my debt to Rickie Dammann for his stimulating and congenial supervision of the thesis which forms the basis of this book and to Robert Bernasconi. Both gave more than generously of their invaluable time and knowledge. I would also like to take this opportunity of thanking Colin Middleton Murry who has been a guide and inspiration almost since I began to read.

I should also like to acknowledge my indebtedness to the Librarian and staff of the University of Sussex Library and the British Library and especially to Christina Gee and Roberta Davis of the Keats Memorial Library in Hampstead. The untiring assistance and knowledge of library staff is taken for granted but no study of this kind would be possible without it.

Also, I should like to thank the staff at Harvester Press for putting up with me as this, my first book, went through the press.

1

Watcher of the Skies

One of the most striking things about the little volume of poems which Keats published in 1817 is the clear evidence it provides, even at this early date, of Keats' extraordinarily rapid development. This little book, which Keats called simply *Poems*, consists of work done between the spring of 1815 and the end of 1816. In it we can see clearly a movement from 'a few raw sonnets'[1] to the more assured and unmistakably Keatsian mastery of 'Sleep and Poetry'. This progress is equally a development of many of Keats' poetic concerns, which although already clearly visible here are usually dealt with by reference to later works and the letters. The composition of these poems covered a quarter of Keats' creative life, and his head is already 'pregnant with poetic lore'.[2] As a last thought immediately prior to publication Keats added a note apologising for 'the Short Pieces in the middle of the Book as well as some of the Sonnets', because they 'were written at an earlier period than the rest of the Poems'.[3] This is an indication that Keats recognised their inferiority. Prior to these inferior productions there is nothing at all.

Keats awoke to the power of poetry surprisingly late—not until his nineteenth year—and the catalyst seems to have been Spenser. Brown wrote that 'Keats was ignorant of his birthright until he had completed his eighteenth year' and that 'it was the "Faerie Queene" that awakened his genius'.[4] Charles Cowden Clarke, Keats' teacher and friend, remembers reading him the 'Epithalamion' and seeing his face transfigured with pleasure. His expression as he listened to 'the more passionate passages' was 'ecstatic'.[5] Cowden Clarke did his utmost to foster this new interest in Keats, but his own feelings for literature were limited. He was a typical well-read young man of his day and, because of this, Keats' introduction to poetry was via the classics of the ancient world and the classical tastes of the eighteenth century. While still at school he had begun a prose translation of the 'Aeneid'. The headmaster, John Cowden Clarke, had given him a copy of Ovid's '*Metamorphoses*'. He already had a copy of '*Paradise Lost*' and possessed the works of Terence and Horace. Charles Cowden Clarke consolidated this tendency. His poetic ideals remained within the limits set by Johnson's *Lives of the English Poets*. Thus Keats' immediate attraction to the works of Spenser was the first sign of an independent mind and implied an early renunciation of the clearly defined forms and strict moral attitudes of eighteenth-century verse, which parallels his later renunciation of Milton.[6]

His intense reading in the classical strain seems not to have inspired him as Spenser did. Even in the earliest poem to which he was prepared to admit—An 'Imitation of Spenser'—which was rather an imitation of Spenser's eighteenth-century imitators, shows Keats freeing himself from rational cleverness, from verses 'cut by feet'.[7]

These signs of early independence were more surprising in view of one of the many friends Keats had at this time who were members of his brother George's circle in London, George Felton Mathew. Mathew was about the same age as Keats, and they were 'both inclined to literature', although their characters, at least according to Mathew's later account, seem to have been very different. He speaks of Keats' 'great confidence in himself' and of his 'fine flow of animal spirits', but says of himself that he was 'languid and melancholy'.[8] Mathew's tastes were similar to Clarke's but lacked Clarke's width. Unlike Clarke, however, Mathew wrote verse himself, and Keats spent happy evenings with him reading their own compositions to each other. They were a 'brotherhood in song'.[9] But Keats soon outgrew Mathew's love of Wieland's 'Oberon', as he did Mathew's affection for Ossian and Mary Tighe. In October 1816 Mathew wrote his 'Lines to a Poetical Friend', pleading with Keats not to let the rigours of his apprenticeship interfere with his writing of poetry. But Keats was thinking of romantic epics:

> Of courteous knights-errant, and high-mettled steeds;
> Of forests enchanted, and marvellous streams;
> Of bridges, and castles, and desperate deeds;
> And all the bright fictions of fanciful dreams[10]

But these 'strange tales of the elf and the fay'[11] were being drowned for Keats by the day-to-day horrors of hospital life. Poetry meant more to him than mere escape from these realities, and verse romances which dream of chivalry were incompatible with hospital attendance:

the coy muse, with me she would not live
In this dark city[12]

far different cares
Beckon me sternly from soft 'Lydian airs'[13]

Life—reality—was calling Keats away from the 'soft "Lydian airs" '
which Mathew so loved. Another influence was already at work on
him. Through Charles Cowden Clarke he had been introduced to
Leigh Hunt, who was famous not only as a poet but also through his
involvements in the politics of the day. Hunt had a genius for
hospitality, and his circle included some of the great literary figures of
the time—Charles Lamb, William Hazlitt and William Godwin
among a number of lesser figures. Keats' relationship with this circle
was a key influence on his early development. It was through Hunt
that Keats met Benjamin Robert Haydon, who was thought by many
to be one of the great painters of the age. Hunt also introduced him to
Joseph Severn, who was to be at his bedside in Rome when he died. To
a young man taking his first steps in the literary world, this inclusion in
the circle of Hunt's friends could not fail to be influential. Severn
wrote that it 'intoxicated him with an excess of enthusiasm'.[14] The
change in Keats was visible, not only to Mathew but to many of Keats'
friends. From this point on he was determined to become a poet and
began to consider himself one. He began to dress poetically, à la
Byron, and it is of some significance that, from the spring of 1816 on,
the subject of Keats' poetry, what it was about, became increasingly
the writing of poetry itself. Subject and form were coalescing.

This movement towards being a poet was given a tremendous boost
when his poem 'To Solitude' was published in the 5 May issue of
Hunt's *Examiner*. It was the first visible evidence that his ambitions
might be realised. It certainly resulted in a further shift away from
Mathew, who detested Hunt's aims, and towards Hunt himself. For
an unknown such as Keats to associate with the renowned leader of the
Cockney School of poetry, editor of the *Examiner*, a man famed for his
radical views both of poetry and politics, must have seemed like the
realisation of a dream. It is clear that Hunt recognised the promise of
Keats' work. When Cowden Clarke showed him some of his
manuscripts, Hunt said that he could 'never forget the impression
made upon me by the exuberant specimens of genuine though young
poetry', and Cowden Clarke was 'not prepared for the unhesitating

and prompt admiration that broke forth'.[15] On 1 December 1816 Hunt included in the *Examiner* an article whose object was 'to notice three young poets', and these three were Reynolds, Shelley and Keats. In this article Hunt mentions the manuscripts which Clarke had given him: 'A set of manuscripts was handed to us the other day, and fairly surprised us with the truth of their ambition'.[16]

Hunt confirmed Keats' love of nature and of the particular against the generalising restrictions of classical art which Mathew preferred, and he consolidated this by reference to the Elizabethan poets Chapman, Sandys, John Fletcher and Spenser himself. And, of course, to Wordsworth. Hunt had taken on board Wordsworth's demand that poetry should speak of experience and do so in the common language of men: 'Pope and the French school of versification ... have mistaken mere smoothness for harmony ... because their ears were only sensible of a marked and uniform regularity'; whereas Hunt was asking for: 'a freer spirit of versification ... [and] a free and idiomatic cast of language ... The proper language of poetry is in fact nothing different from that of real life, and depends for its dignity upon the strength and sentiment of what it speaks.'[17]

The problem was that Hunt, not being Wordsworth, was unable to put this theory into practice and, although his long poem 'The Story of Rimini' demonstrates the possibilities of a more relaxed structure, it does so by destroying the syntax and usage of common man. Hunt, like Chapman, whose translation of Homer was the instigation of Keats' first great poem, didn't hesitate to change grammar, coin new words, interchange parts of speech and a lot more besides, but in doing so he forgot his own dictum that poetry should be free of '*mere* vulgarisms and fugitive phrases, which are the cant of ordinary discourse'.[18]

Keats, however, adored it. Whatever criticisms may be held against it, it is a fast-moving tale, its imagery is sensuous and colourful, it is exciting and full of life. More than this, it succeeded in freeing myth from the strictures of neo-classic versifying. Hunt had accepted Wordsworth's arguments about myth in the 'Excursion' and, by extracting them from their neo-classic prison, had freed them as a valid subject for poetry. Anyway, it was enough for Keats that it was Hunt's work. He was determined to try and emulate it. In the 1817 volume we have his two early efforts in this vein. They show Hunt's influence in their slack rhythms, their untidy diction and their eroticism, but the saving grace of 'Rimini', the speed of its narrative, is replaced by static description. In the first of these Keats twice states his determination to 'tell a tale of chivalry'.[19] He knows clearly enough what he wants to do, but it goes against the grain, and he calls on Spenser for inspiration:

> Spencer! thy brows are arched, open, kind,
> And come like a clear sun-rise to my mind;
> And always does my heart with pleasure dance,
> When I think on thy noble countenance[20]

Calling on his:

> gentle spirit to hover nigh
> My daring steps[21]

As well as feeling humble towards Spenser, he also feels guilty in trying to follow that 'bright path of light' already traced by Hunt, who will:

> tell thee that my prayer is very meek;
> That I will follow with due reverence,
> And start with awe at mine own strange pretence[22]

Here, after this unusual show of meekness, the text ends. Keats called it merely a 'Specimen of an Induction to a Poem', and by this title accepted his failure graciously. But he was still as determined as ever to produce a 'tale of chivalry', and for his second attempt picks on the story of Calidore from the 'Faerie Queene'. But, once again, he is writing from example, making an intellectual effort and thus destroying his own voice. His example here is more clearly 'The Story of Rimini' and Hunt himself, who Keats refers to as Libertas. Keats speaks of himself as one:

> who, of late, had ta'en sweet forest walks
> With him who elegantly chats, and talks—
> The wrong'd Libertas,—who has told you stories
> Of laurel chaplets, and Apollo's glories;
> Of troops chivalrous prancing through a city,

> And tearful ladies made for love, and pity:
> With many else that I have never known[23]

In 'Calidore', the concrete trappings of chivalry—'the torches' glare',[24] the 'noble steeds',[25] the 'armour ... dexterously wrought'[26]—is done well enough, but Keats never gets to its soul. It remains superficial because it meant little to him. His conscious ambition to write poetry, and poetry of a certain kind, deadened his inspiration and left a void at the heart of the poem. Finally, as Calidore says of himself, it shows only:

> The large-eyed wonder, the ambitious heat
> Of the aspiring boy[27]

Keats aim was immortal fame which would enable his spirit to: 'lofty converse hold with aftertime'.[28] In 'To My Brother George' he lists the influence which his poetry might have:

> The patriot shall feel
> My stern alarum, and unsheath his steel;
> Or, in the senate thunder out my numbers
> To startle princes from their easy slumbers.
> The sage will mingle with each moral theme
> My happy thoughts sententious; he will teem
> With lofty periods when my verses fire him,
> And then I'll stoop from heaven to inspire him.
> Lays have I left of such a dear delight
> That maids will sing them on their bridal night[29]

This imitative telling of tales aimed at a future immortality was too conscious, and Keats was steadily coming to recognise that this was a limitation.

The writing of these early 'failures' were Keats' first lesson in creativity—that a poet who consciously directs himself to write according to the example of others or the stylistic canons of his day, even for so high an ideal as immortality, will deny his genius. Keats' entire writing life was continual overcoming of just such restrictions. His concern to use poetry for a purpose, as a tool, as a medium for some purpose beyond itself, was overtaken by a genuine internal mechanism of creativity. Keats was increasingly concerned with the writing of poetry as immediate. He quickly discovered that imitating Hunt or following Hunt's stylistic precepts was a restriction from which he had to rescue himself. The catalyst for this early overcoming was Benjamin Haydon.

Although today Haydon is hardly known, in Keats' day he was considered one of the leading lights in the world of art. Haydon's genius was in persuading others that he was a genius, and he managed to do this mainly through a superabundance of chaotic energy. His own enormous confidence in his work made others believe in it. He was an 'unbending champion' of the Elgin Marbles and active in persuading the British Museum to purchase them.[30] He was constantly compaigning for one thing or another. His many friends took him at his own estimate of himself. In the week that Keats first met Haydon, Hunt compared him in the *Examiner* to Raphael and Michaelangelo. He was:

> Fit to be numbered in succession due
> With Michael, whose idea austerly presses,
> And sweet-souled Raphael[31]

Keats could scarcely have escaped being caught up in this atmosphere of admiration. He includes himself as one of the 'unnumbered souls' who:

> breath out a still applause,
> Proud to behold him in his country's eye[32]

and speaks of being 'very glad ... at thoughts of seeing so soon this glorious Haydon and all his Creation'.[33]

Keats first sight of Haydon's studio could only have consolidated this opinion. It was a small room dominated by Haydon's enormous current project, his painting 'Christ's Entry into Jerusalem', on which he had already been working for over a year. The two men immediately impressed each other. On the morning after their first meeting Keats sent Haydon a sonnet. Writing that 'last evening wraught me up', he addressed Haydon as one:

> whose steadfastness would never take
> A meaner sound than Raphael's whispering

and who:

> will give the world another heart
> And other pulses[34]

This echoes Hunt's assessment. And Haydon, in his own self-centred way, was equally impressed by Keats. He says that he had 'read one or two of his sonnets and formed a very high idea of his genius'.[35] He was 'really and truly the man after my own heart', one to 'sympathise with to comprehend me'.[36] Haydon was not the sort of man to keep these feelings to himself, and he must have helped to confirm Keats' belief in his own promise. Keats often visited the studio to watch Haydon at work, and they spent many hours in intense discussion on art and poetry. During these meetings they must often have sat together reading Shakespeare aloud, and Haydon later stated that he 'enjoyed Shakespeare with John Keats more than with any other human creature'.[37] At this time Keats also went to view the Elgin Marbles, which struck him with their energy, their accuracy and their vivacity. The marbles made him feel:

> Like a sick eagle looking at the sky[38]

He describes them as 'of godlike hardship'[39] and an 'incarnate Delight'.[40]

Haydon's chaotic, bull-necked energy rang a chord in Keats, and he began to draw away from Hunt just as surely as he had earlier drawn towards him and away from Mathew. Hunt's preference was for the private and sentimental, and he put Ariosto and Tasso above Homer, and Spenser above Shakespeare. Haydon, on the other hand, preferred Homer's masculine power to the control shown by Ariosto and Tasso—the strength of the heroic over weakness and effeminacy. Above all, he worshipped Shakespeare.

Keats began to see Hunt's love of the 'playing of nymph in woods and fountains',[41] of 'enchanted grots'[42] and the 'visions' of a 'high romance'[43]—the 'realm ... of Flora, and old Pan'[44]—as an escape, as a failure to face up to the genuine demands of creativity, demands which Keats was increasingly prepared to accept. This movement is clearly visible in 'Sleep and Poetry'. He states unmistakably that:

> the realm I'll pass
> Of Flora, and old Pan[45]

and that he will pass them:

> for a nobler life
> Where I may find the agonies, the strife
> Of human hearts[46]

In the first of these realms he luxuriates in the visions of fancy. He can:

> sleep in the grass,
> Feed upon apples red, and strawberries,
> And choose each pleasure that my fancy sees[47]

But he must 'bid these joys farewell';[48] he must put aside the indulgence of fancy that he had learnt from Hunt, because such indulgence is never poesy. Poesy is something else. In 'Sleep and Poetry' Keats strives to tell us what it is and, in doing so, enters upon his birthright.

Nobler than fancy is the search for:

> the agonies, the strife
> Of human hearts[49]

which is the strife of the heart of the poet who, recognising his genuis, sees in the very moment of recognition that his genius involves its own sublimation. The poet is a charioteer who:

> Looks out upon the winds with glorious fear
> . . . .
> Most awefully intent
> The driver of those steeds is forward bent,
> And seems to listen[50]

The paradox of the power of genius and its humility is already there. The horseman who drives 'his steeds with streamy manes'[51] through the heavens, at the same time looks ahead with 'fear'—but a fear that is glorious. And though he is 'forward bent', it is to 'listen'. The charioteer is supreme and attentive at the same time, and Keats wishes:

> that I might know
> All that he writes with such a hurrying glow[52]

But these visions, of themselves, are inadequate. They vanish and:

> in their stead
> A sense of real things comes doubly strong[53]

Keats feels that this reality:

> like a muddy stream would bear along
> My soul to nothingness[54]

The fear that reality—the hospital wards in which he was spending his days—would drive away vision instead of reinforcing it, is still strong. He determines that he will:

> strive
> Against all doubtings, and will keep alive
> The thought of that same chariot, and the strange
> Journey it went[55]

This insight inevitably made him see the derivative, fanciful nature of most poetry. He writes that today:

> the high
> Imagination cannot freely fly
> As she was want of old[56]

because poets had failed to arrive at these new insights:

> ye were dead
> To things ye knew not of [57]

Poetry had become mere technique. Poets now:

> were closely wed
> To musty laws lined out with wretched rule
> And compass vile: so that ye taught a school
> Of dolts to smooth, inlay, and clip, and fit,

> Easy was the task:
> A thousand handicraftsmen wore the mask
> Of Poesy.[58]

Poetry is never merely a technique that can be learnt, nor is it the mere power of the charioteer, because along with the handicraftsmen there have been poets of power:

> In truth we've had
> Strange thunders from the potency of song[59]

These have even been:

> Mingled indeed with what is sweet and strong,
> From majesty[60]

In other words, they have fulfilled Keats' demand that poetry should involve an attentive strength, and that they should do this without any investment of ideas, without any ulterior motivation, because:

> in clear truth the themes
> Are ugly clubs, the Poets Polyphemes
> Disturbing the grand sea. [61]

Poetry is never the communication of a theme, never the medium by which an idea is passed on. Any such didactic purpose would be too active, too much in control of itself and thus, even if powerful, would be insufficiently attentive:

> strength alone though of the Muses born
> Is like a fallen angel[62]

True poesy, on the other hand, is something else:

> A drainless shower
> Of light is poesy; 'tis the supreme power;
> 'Tis might half-slumb'ring on its own right arm.
> The very archings of her eye-lids charm

A thousand willing agents to obey,
And still she governs with the mildest sway[63]

The poet, in rejecting both the affirmation of ideas and the self-affirmation of strength still accepts the strength demanded of a supreme power—which governs him with 'the mildest sway'—because he is willing to be governed. Poesy is pregnant with itself and expresses nothing but itself. It is, as itself, immediate. Never a form which mediates a content, its form is its content. It is its own potential, and as potential to itself makes no demands on the poet to exert himself, but rather uses him who obeys willingly. Poesy is never about anything, even poesy, but simply is itself and thus *is*; exists. It belongs merely to itself. It is its own:

'Tis might half-slumb'ring on its own right arm.

This extraordinary passage is almost unique at this point of Keats' life. It stands out as Keatsian against the remainder of the 1817 volume with all its echoes of Spencer, Wordworth, Hunt and Mathew. It is inexplicable for the very reason that it is about itself and can therefore only stand as itself. The remainder of the poem is more explicable. It has themes, or rather Keats' only theme from this point on: the writing of poetry. He tells us that thematic writing forgets:

the great end
Of poesy, that it should be a friend
To soothe the cares, and lift the thoughts of man[64]

and that:

they shall be accounted poet-kings
Who simply tell the most heart-easing things.[65]

Yet this simplistic notion of poetry is not the reality but merely 'delightful hopes' when:

th' imagination
Into most lovely labyrinths will be gone[66]

This is Hunt speaking again and is not poetry but 'prose in verse'.[67] It is thematic and lacks strength, and Keats immediately excuses himself. He is still young, and he asks:

> Will not some say that I presumptuously
> Have spoken? that from hastening disgrace
> 'Twere better far to hide my foolish face?[68]

But he answers that even:

> If I do hide myself, it sure shall be
> In the very fane, the light of Poesy[69]

This is so because poetry is not a pastime and because those:

> who, athirst to gain
> A noble end, are thirsty every hour[70]

Keats is as yet young and says of himself:

> though I am not wealthy in the dower
> Of spanning wisdom; though I do not know
> The shiftings of the mighty winds that blow
> Hither and thither all the changing thoughts
> Of man[71]

and, above all:

> though no great minist'ring reason sorts
> Out the dark mysteries of human souls
> To clear conceiving: yet there ever rolls
> A vast idea before me[72]

The vast idea rolls before the young poet in spite of his lack of conceptual knowledge and in spite, even, of his growing conviction that it will never be available. Of this, at the very least, he is sure:

> I glean
> Therefrom my liberty; thence too I've seen

> The end and aim of Poesy. 'Tis clear
> As anything most true[73]

Keats has fallen back from his conviction of poetry as 'might half-slumb'ring on its own right arm', away from the conviction of poetry as that which commands obedience of its willing agents, whom it governs with the mildest sway. The vast idea, which he here takes to be the end and aim of poesy, is available to effort—tremendous, poetic effort but effort, activity, nonetheless. He now sees the end and aim of poesy as:

> An ocean dim, sprinkled with many an isle[74]

which 'spreads awfully' before him.[75] It is the immense effort needed to attain it that makes a 'coward' of him:

>   How much toil!
> How many days! What desperate turmoil!
> Ere I can have explored its wildernesses.
> Ah, what a task![76]

This contest in Keats' conception of creativity between poetry as task, as effort, and his growing conviction of it as a diligent attention dogged his path throughout the composition of 'Endymion' and could be said to be the undercurrent to his whole poetic life. It certainly results in some of the inconsistencies so easily noticed in the poem. But at this moment, Keats reaches a sort of plateau of compromise between the two. He achieves this with the help of the legend of Diana and the inspiration of the moon. The moon was a significant symbol for Keats. The ghostly, watery glimmer of moonlight transforms the world in which it shines into a mystery in which imagination can dream. Diana, the goddess of the moon, transforms the world into poetry and does so through her love of the poet's solitude. Because she wanders alone herself, she can be 'a lover of loneliness, and wandering'[77] and this love creates poetry:

> Thee must I praise above all other glories
> That smile on us to tell delightful stories
> For what has made the sage or poet write
> But the fair paradise of Nature's light[78]

Diana is a 'maker of sweet poets'[79] by granting them life in her light. She brings them:

> Shapes from the invisible world, unearthly singing
> From out the middle air[80]

and this gift is granted to the poet who has 'burst our mortal bars':

> Into some wond'rous region he had gone[81]

to win Diana through love. Love is the gift which grants the poet his immortality. He has 'burst his mortal bars' in order:

> To search for thee, divine Endymion![82]

Endymion was 'a Poet, sure a lover too'[83] who breathed 'a hymn from Dian's temple'[84] and recognised that her lover needed requiting:

> The Poet wept at her so piteous fate,
> Wept that such beauty could be desolate:
> So in fine wrath some golden sounds he won,
> And gave meek Cynthia her Endymion.[85]

The marriage, the synthesis, of these two is the very act of creativity, and Keats asks:

> for three words of honey, that I might
> Tell but one wonder of thy bridal night![86]

His wandering spirit dares to think that their union might produce a poet and that he might be that poet:

> I cannot tell the greater blisses,
> That follow'd thine and thy dear shepherd's kisses:
> Was there a Poet born?[87]

In this moment of daring, the poem breaks off:

> My wand'ring spirit must no further soar.[88]

But this very conception of the poetical relation between mortals and the mysteries of Diana is the subject that Keats takes up again in 'Endymion'.

2

A Den to Save the Whole

By 1817 Keats felt that the time had come to compose a 'Poem'. When Keats uses this word in the singular and with a capital 'P', he almost invariably means a substantial, extended piece of writing. When referring to his shorter pieces, he tends to be dismissive. The 'Epistle to Mathew' is called a 'sheet or two of Verses',[1] a sonnet is 'a Sonnet'[2] and an ode is an 'Ode'.[3] At other times he speaks of 'doggrel',[4] 'Lines'[5] or 'a song',[6] 'a Morning work at most'.[7] In the cancelled preface to 'Endymion' he refers to his 1817 volume as 'a little book of verses'.[8]

'Endymion' itself, on the other hand, is consistently referred to as a Poem. ' "Not begun at all 'till half done" so according to that I have not begun my Poem ... I revoke my Promise of finishing my Poem by the Autumn'.[9] 'I am proceeding at a pretty good rate with a Poem'.[10] Again, in the cancelled preface, he always uses 'Poem' to refer to a substantial piece of work, either 'Endymion' itself or, when 'Endymion' has failed, to 'a new Poem', 'Hyperion', with which he hopes to redeem himself.[11] In a letter to Bailey (Oct 1817) Keats copies out part of a letter to his brother George which has since been lost and in which he asks: 'Did our great Poets ever write short Pieces?' and identifies the difficulties of extended composition and the reasons for making the attempt:[12]

> The high Idea I have of poetical fame makes me think I see it towering to[o] high above me. At any rate I have no right to talk until Endymion is finished—it will be a test, a trial of my Powers of Imagination and chiefly of my invention which is a rare thing indeed—by which I must make 4000 Lines of one bare circumstance and fill them with Poetry; and when I consider that this is a great task, and that when done it will take me but a dozen paces towards the Temple of Fame—it makes me say—God forbid that I should be without such a task!'[13]

The composition of 'Endymion'—of a 'Poem'—which will place him 'in the Mouth of Fame' is a task which 'has grown so monstrously beyond my seeming Power of attainment'.[14] Keats describes himself as 'one that "gathers Samphire dreadful trade" the Cliff of Poesy Towers above me'.[15] Poetry, poesy, is seen as a task to be undertaken in which powers of invention and imagination will have to be used.

The nature of poetry is to be found in a long Poem because 'a long Poem is a test of Invention which I take to be the Polar Star of Poetry, as Fancy is the Sails, and Imagination the Rudder.'[16] Such a Poem, in which the nature of poetry really manifests itself, is here perceived as a craft which has be steered skilfully into port. Fame is the spur. 'The Trumpet of Fame is a tower of Strength the ambitious bloweth it and is safe'.[17]

'Poetical fame'[18] spurs Keats on to compose a Poem, one which will call on all his powers of imagination, invention and fancy. He had spent the winter of 1816/17 reading Elizabethan poetry, the 'lovely tales that we have heard or read',[19] and these acted as an example for the retelling of those myths of ancient Greece with sufficient latitude to allow for description, adventure, philosophy and allegory. But this Keats calls a 'task'—a test, a trial of his powers, a cliff to be climbed—and for this he has to be drawn on by ambition for fame.

From the start Keats planned to produce four books of 1,000 lines each and to sit down daily to work. Immediately after the opening lines of the first book, he sets out his timetable:

> I will begin
> . . . .
> Now while the early budders are just new,
> . . . .
>   and, as the year
> Grows lush in juicy stalks, I'll smoothly steer
> My little boat
> . . . .
>   let Autumn bold,
> . . . .
> Be all about me when I make an end[20]

All this is evidence of effort, of working at a composition in the hope that his powers will be adequate to a task which he feels to be 'monstrously beyond my seeming Power of attainment'.[21] But he keeps at it. At the beginning of May he writes to Leigh Hunt: 'I began my Poem about a Fortnight since and have done some every day except travelling ones ... I see ... nothing but continual uphill Journeying'.[22] and the next day he wrote to Haydon:

> I read and write about eight hours a day. There is an old saying 'well begun is half done'—'tis a bad one. I would use instead—'Not begun at all 'till half done' so according to that I have not begun my Poem ... I do begin arduously where I leave off, notwithstanding occasional depressions.[23]

On the following day he received some bad news about money matters from George, and this disrupts his working pattern:

> I revoke my Promise of finishing my Poem by the Autumn which I should have done had I gone on as I have done—but I cannot write while my spirit is fevered in a contrary direction ... I feel that I am not in a Mood to write any to day; and it appears that the loss of it is the beginning of all sorts of irregularities.[24]

In the middle of May he is writing to his publishers:

> I went day by day at my Poem for a Month at the end of which time the other day I found my Brain so overwrought that I had neither Rhyme nor reason in it—so was obliged to give up for a few days—I hope soon to be able to resume my work—I have endeavoured to do so once or twice but to no Purpose—instead of Poetry I have a swimming in my head—And feel all the effects of Mental Debauch—lowness of Spirits—anxiety to go on without the Power to do so which does not at all tend to my ultimate Progression—However tomorrow I will begin my next Month.[25]

There are no extant letters for June, July or August, barring one to his publishers asking for an advance. On 10 September he wrote to his sister from Oxford, where he was clossetted with Bailey studying poetry—especially that of Wordsworth. The third book of 'Endymion' is unmistakably the result of these academic weeks:

> We lead very industrious lives he in general Studies and I in proceeding at a pretty good rate with a Poem which I hope you will see early in the next year ... I have been writing very hard lately even till an utter incapacity came on, and I feel it now about my head: ... I shall stop

here till I have finished the 3rd Book of my Story; which I hope will be accomplish'd in at most three weeks from today.[26]

Bailey described Keats' life at Oxford:

He sat down to his task, which was about fifty lines a day, with his paper before him, and wrote with as much regularity and apparently with as much ease as he wrote his letters. Indeed, he quite acted up to the principle he lays down, 'that if Poetry comes not as naturally as the leaves of a tree, it had better not come at all'. Sometimes he fell short of his allotted task, but not often, and he would make it up another day. But he never forced himself.[27]

This regular timetable and Bailey's close interest and encouragement paid off. On 21 September Keats is able to write to Reynolds: 'I am getting on famous with my third Book—have written 800 lines thereof, and hope to finish it next week—Bailey likes what I have done very much'.[28] And a week later he tells Hayden that the third book is finished: 'You will be glad to hear that within these last three weeks I have written 1000 lines—which are the third Book of my Poem'.[29] He is not entirely satisfied with the result:

My Ideas with respect to it I assure you are very low—and I would write the subject thoroughly again ... Rome was not built in a Day and all the good I expect from my employment this summer is the fruit of Experience.[30]

At the end of October, a full month later, he is still struggling with the beginning of the fourth book. He writes to Bailey:

I don't suppose I've written as many Lines as you have read Volumes or at least Chapters since I saw you. However, I am in a fair way now to come to a conclusion in at least three weeks when I assure you I shall be glad to dismount for a Month or two—although I'll keep as tight a reign as possible till then nor suffer myself to sleep.[31]

He then quotes to Bailey the rather academic opening lines of Book IV and, continuing the same letter a week later after completing the Indian Maiden's song, he writes: 'You must forgive although I have only written 300 Lines—they would have been five but I have been obliged to go to town'.[32] At the end of November he tells Bailey he needs 'a spur to wind up my Poem, of which there is wanting 500 Lines'.[33] The work has been going slowly, and Keats has been incorporating smaller poems into the structure. 'O Sorrow', the first part of the 'Indian Maiden's Song' is included separately in a letter to Jane Reynolds. There is a clear break between this and the 'Triumph of Bacchus', which is a more substantial ninety-one lines in length. The texture of the long Poem is showing signs of fracturing.

It is clear that the composition of 'Endymion' was a strain for Keats. It was a task which he felt he had to complete so as to realise his overt, stated ambition of being a Poet with a capital 'P'. He stuck closely to his intention of writing four books of 1,000 lines each.[34] 'Endymion' remains the only long Poem that Keats completed. In the rejected preface to the Poem he wrote: 'Before I began I had no inward feel of being able to finish; and as I proceeded my steps were all uncertain'.[35] He had the 'anxiety to go on without the Power to do so'.[36] Also in the rejected preface he writes: 'This Poem, must rather be consider'd as an endeavour than a thing accomplished'.[37] In the printed preface this becomes: 'a feverish attempt, rather than a dead accomplished'.[38]

The key word here is 'endeavour'. Keats had yet to learn 'never to write for the sake of writing, or making a poem'.[39] Composition as endeavour, as a 'test ... of invention'[40] leads to faults. He feels guilty of presenting 'Endymion' to the public 'knowing it to be so faulty' and feeling that further endeavour might improve it. 'In duty to the Public I should have kept it back a year or two'.[41] Yet he realises at the same moment that any such 'attempt' or 'endeavour' at improvement will prove fundamentally useless. In the published preface he writes:

> The two first books, and indeed the two last, I feel sensible are not of such completion as to warrant their passing the press; nor should they if I thought a year's castigation would do them any good;—it will not: the foundations are too sandy.[42]

Attempt, endeavour, task, test of invention, a year's castigation—driven on by ambition and the desire to write a 'Poem', Keats forced himself on. Yet by the time these prefaces were written in the spring of 1818, he had come to realise that poesy cannot be created 'from a knowledge of what is to be arrived at'.[43] On the contrary: 'It is easier to think what Poetry should be than to write it ... if Poetry comes not as naturally as the Leaves to a tree, it had better not come at all'.[44]

Thinking is somehow alien to and easier than creating. Thinking is an effort which produces a result, an effort which is known to have succeeded by its result. In creativity there is no such continuity of effort and result. The effort of thought is a task, an attempt, an endeavour, whereas creation comes 'naturally'.[45] For Keats it seems almost to depend on a lack of thought, on 'half-knowledge' in which 'Beauty overcomes every consideration, or rather obliterates all consideration'[46] He writes to Bailey that one thing in particular has:

> increased my Humility and capability of submission and that is this truth—Men of Genius are great as certain ethereal Chemicals operating on the Mass of neutral intellect—but they have not any individuality, any determined Character—I would call the top and head of those who have a proper Self Men of Power.[47]

Thus a 'capability of submission', a lack of individuality, is compared to the proper Self of Men of Power. Keats considered his failure in 'Endymion' to have been the failure of a Man of Power. His ambition to gain fame as a poet gave him the 'anxiety to go on' but 'without the Power to do so'.[48] His failure was failure of Power, of Self. To aim consciously towards a result was the wrong foundation for poetry; correcting a poem written on such a foundation would do no good—the foundation itself was 'too sandy'.[49]

This is the lesson Keats began to learn from the writing of 'Endymion'. Men of Power who invoke Self to organise and control existence are never men of genius who have the 'capability of submission'. In a letter to Bailey (November 1817) Keats differentiates carefully between the two for the first time. Men of genius are intellectually neutral, 'they have not any individuality, any determined character', and this neutral intellect is operated on by 'certain ethereal Chemicals'. This neutral, passive intellect is the reverse of that of Men of Power 'who have a proper Self'. The keys to this neutral intellect are passion and imagination which operate beyond the controls of a thinking which wants to extract knowledge from experience—to subsume experience to knowledge.

The distinction between thinking and feeling was not, of course, original to Keats but a major concern of the Romantic movement. Their approach was no longer one of trusting to thought to explain emotions, but the reverse: 'many excellent philosophers have now shown that thought is but a faculty of feeling'.[50] This reverse from the priority of reason to that of feeling was a reaction against the rational attitude, which took all knowledge to be derived from experience. Locke, for instance, argued that there exist no innate ideas or principles, and he spoke out against putting one's trust in the logical syllogism or ungrounded generalisations: 'We reason about particulars'.[51] Knowledge comes only from sensations and, following Berkeley, the mind can form no conclusion beyond the evidence supplied to it by sense perception. Empiricism, having once deposed the mind as a strictly rational instrument completely in control of its kingdom, had increasingly to resort to feeling to replace it.

Feeling is for them more basic than neo-classic reason, first because its immediacy allows a more spontaneous reaction to sensations, and secondly because it refuses to pre-empt a mental response by limiting it to any category or set of categories. Feeling is free and thus allows access to naunces of signification and the relations between them to which any logical approach would be impervious. 'There is a correspondence between certain external forms of Nature, and certain affections of the Mind, that may be felt, but cannot always be explained'.[52]

Reality is, above all else, characterised by flux and change. By reasoning *about* it the mind abstracts and categorises, producing statements about this flux which impose upon it a rigidity and order belonging not to the empirical reality itself but to the method applied to it. The neo-classic conception of the world sees it as being governed by a set of laws, and the job of art is to reflect this natural order:

> Romantic poetry, on the other hand, is the expression of a secret attraction to a chaos which lies concealed ... The former is more simple, clear, and like to nature in the self-existent perfection of her separate works. The latter ... approaches more to the secret of the universe. For Conception can only comprise each object separately; *feeling* perceives all in all at one and the same time.[53]

This distinction between actively applying a rationale to perceptions and allowing the full flow of their natural complexity—a complexity which it is beyond us to grasp in its entirety—implies a change in the attitude we take up towards sensations. If we no longer limit interpretation to the mediation of some objective method, then we must submit to its immediacy, with all the subsequent complexity and levels of uncertainty, allowing it to take hold of us, flow through us and become us. To combat reason as interpretative method, the

Romantics substituted sympathy. In Romantic writings it is often stated that the imagination is able to subdue itself in a sympathetic act of identification with the object of its contemplation. The spontaneous feelings of the poet overflow into the objects of sense uncontrolled by reason.

However, there is in these feelings a distinct touch of reticence, a feeling that the imagination is itself exerting its own special kind of control over the world it sees. It is, of course, in no way analytic or objective in the way that reason is. Nevertheless, it is there. The poet's feelings and the quality of his imagination overflow into and transform the world he senses. Hazlitt writes that 'poetry ... in describing natural objects ... impregnates sensible impressions with the forms of fancy'.[54] Here, the poet's ego is not dissolved by the object it contemplates; it merely imposes itself in the form of feeling rather than that of reason, the subjective rather than the putative objective. Coleridge is quite explicit: 'Whilst it recalls the sights and sounds that had accompanied the occasions of the original passions, poetry impregnates them with an interest not their own'.[55] Hazlitt writes that the feelings of agitation fear and love all 'distort and magnify the object'.[56] And he gives as an example Iachamo saying:

> The flame o' th' taper
> Bows toward her, and would under-peep her lids
> To see the enclosed lights[57]

He explains that this is a 'passionate interpretation of the motion of the flame to accord with the speaker's own feelings'.[58] Or again, as Coleridge puts it at the conclusion of a famous passage of the *Biographia Literaria*: 'images ... become proofs of original genius only as far as they are modified by a predominant passion; or ... when a human or intellectual life is transferred to them from the poet's own spirit'.[59]

The movement here is from the poet towards the object. The description of the poet's ego may have radically changed, but the ego itself has remained intact. The basic conception is one of empathy—the *einfühlung* of German Romanticism—and empathy can only operate between two things. This proved useful in the field of ethics; a man's empathy for another could modify his egotism and give a more understanding moral sense.

But Keats, during November and December of 1817, seems to be moving beyond this and towards the notion of the poet as receptive and Self-less. In the letter to Bailey he writes of 'the authenticity of the imagination':

> I am certain of nothing but of the holiness of the Heart's affections and the truth of Imagination—what the imagination seizes as Beauty must be truth—whether it existed before or not—for I have the same Idea of all our Passions as of Love they are all in their sublime, creative of essential Beauty.[60]

These are, perhaps, the best known lines from Keats' letters, and they are the last occasion in the letters that creativity is taken to be active in the way Hazlitt and Coleridge understood it—a movement of the imagination towards truth and beauty. The imagination 'seizes', the passions are creative. But we can, perhaps, pinpoint here the key moment of a speculation: passions and love are 'affection' and are 'holy'. What is holy, is so wholly. The heart's affections are both that which affects the heart and that which the heart affects—both active and passive. The imagination 'seizes', but not in the same way as reason understands, for what it seizes, it seizes as holy—as there wholly—and the 'consequitive reasoning' of 'even the greatest Philosopher' arrives at its goal only by 'putting aside numerous objections', by a process of exclusion—'and yet', Keats insists, 'it must be',[61] otherwise this totally passive grant of poetry by a faith entirely beyond reason would be morally neutral. As Keats later insisted, indolence—dreaming—is not mere passivity but the diligence of identity. But he is not yet at that stage. 'The Chamber of Maiden Thought', of 'consequitive reasoning',[62] 'becomes gradually darken'd and at the same time on all sides of it many doors are set open—but all dark—all leading to dark passages—we see not the ballance of good and evil. We are in a mist. *We* are now in that state'.[63] This darkening of 'the light and the atmosphere'—of reason—is the result of experience, of 'convincing one's nerves that the world is full of Misery and Heartbreak, Pain Sickness and oppression'.[64] What Keats is already struggling with in this early letter to Bailey is the passivity of identity, and how the poet who passively receives poetry as a gift can be other than morally neutral. What, in terms of creativity, *is* an identity that merely receives passively? After all: 'The Imagination may be compared to *Adam's* dream—*he* awoke and found it truth.[65] And a poem of Keats is always a poem of Keats.

Yet Keats is very clear that imagination is not fancy and that poetry does not simply 'impregnate sensible impressions with the forms of fancy',[66] even though he is not at this moment certain what it does do. Imagination, unlike fancy, is holy; that which affects the heart is that which the heart affects. The imagination seizes a beauty which didn't exist before. This is a movement of the passions as the Greeks understood it. Pathos, like its Latin equivalent, *passio*, implies an imposition from without which happens to a man who remains passive.[67] These passions 'are in their sublime creative of essential Beauty', which is there as essence prior to any activity of mind. Activity of mind—'consequitive reasoning'—on its own cannot arrive at a truth without putting aside numerous objections. Imagination is a 'silent working' which repeats what is already there, and this repetition 'comes continually on the spirit with a fine suddenness' which surprises as original. This repetition is 'almost a remembrance':

> The simple imaginative Mind may have its rewards in the repetition of its own silent Working coming continually on the spirit with a fine suddenness—to compare great things with small—have you never by being surprised with an old Melody in a delicious place—by a delicious voice, felt over again your very speculations and surmises at the time it first operated on your Soul—do you not remember forming to yourself the singers face more beautiful than it was possible and yet with the elevation of the Moment you did not think so—even then you were mounted on the Wings of Imagination so high that the Prototype must be here after—that delicious face you will see.[68]

For Bailey, who was at this time trying for his ordination into the priesthood, Keats makes a religious comparison; that this grant of originality for the 'Simple imaginative Mind' must be like heaven; that 'the Prototype must be hereafter': 'We shall enjoy ourselves here after by having what we called happiness on Earth repeated in a finer tone and so repeated'.[69] For all this, Keats refers Bailey to 'my first Book'[70] of 'Endymion', and it must be said that much of it has a clear religious or Wordsworthian tone:

> Wherein lies happiness? In that which becks
> Our ready minds to fellowship divine,
> A fellowship with essence; till we shine,

Full alchemiz'd, and free of space. Behold
The clear religion of heaven.[71]
. . . .
               that moment we have stept
Into a sort of oneness, and our state
Is like a floating spirit's[72]

But this stepping into oneness is not merely the movement of a poet
impelled by fame, it is also a movement guided by heaven. Bacchus is:

              the leaven,
That spreading in this dull and clodded earth
Gives it a touch ethereal—a new birth[73]

Yet this new birth requires the 'solitary thinkings' of the poet which
are directed towards it:

                  such as dodge
Conception to the very bourne of heaven,
Then leave the naked brain[74]

These two moments of a dialectical movement are productive of 'a sort
of oneness' in which:

                     our state
Is like a floating spirit's

But Keats says that there are 'richer entanglements' and that these are:

              enthralments far
More self-destroying, leading, by degrees,
To the chief intensity[75]

The crown of these enthralments:

Is made of love and friendship, and sits high
Upon the forehead of humanity
All its more ponderous and bulky worth
Is friendship, whence there ever issued forth
A steady spendour; but at the tip-top,

> There hangs by unseen film, an orbed drop
> Of light, and that is love: its influence,
> Thrown in our eyes, genders a novel sense,
> At which we start and fret; till in the end,
> Melting into its radiance, we blend,
> Mingle, and so become a part of it[76]

Love genders a novel sense into which we melt. From what has gone before we expect this love to be the love of heaven, of the gods—an external influence. Yet Keats is quite clear that it is rather the love of men and women which:

> although 'tis understood
> The mere commingling of passionate breath[77]

is rather a kissing of human souls without which nothing is possible:

> who, of men, can tell
> That flowers would bloom, or that green fruit would swell
> To melting pulp, that fish would have bright mail,
> The earth its dower of river, wood, and vale,
> The meadows runnels, runnels pebble-stones,
> The seed its harvest, or the lute its tones,
> Tones ravishment, or ravishment its sweet
> If human souls did never kiss and greet?[78]

These are enthralments that are far more self-destroying than a stepping into a sort of oneness, and they are exactly those whose self-destroying is, at the same time, a process of 'self-nourishing'. This does not occur through:

> atomies
> That buzz about our slumbers, like brain-flies,
> Leaving us fancy-sick[79]

It does not occur by the workings of fancy, but by the workings of imagination, which grants or 'genders a novel sense', a self-nourishment. The novel sense and the love which genders it are moments of the same 'into whose radiance we melt' and when we combine with this novel sense, with this radiance:

Life's self is nourish'd by its proper pith[80]

Only by such a self-destroying can a genuine openness, a genuine ripeness, be achieved and the destroyed self be nourished by its proper pith:

> Just so may love, although 'tis understood
> The mere commingling of passionate breath,
> Produce more than our searching witnesseth[81]

Love is its own reward and its ardour is, at the same moment, listless. Keats writes:

> I would be rather be struck dumb,
> Than speak against this ardent listlessness[82]

It is by this passionate acceptance, this 'diligent Indolence',[83] that love is 'creative of essential Beauty' and that the imagination can seize what may not have existed before. This movement of the moments of the heart's affections—that which affects the heart and that which the heart affects—redeems them and makes them whole—holy. It is thus, Keats seems to be saying, that imagination can be authentic. Passion, intensity, love, the heart's affections are self-destroyings which allow life's self to be nourished by its proper pith, which allow for the authenticity of the imagination. Imagination which is authentic, which is autochthonous, which is by and from its own (*auto*), can only be truly nourished by what is proper to it (*proprius*: 'its own'), its proper pith. The recognition by the authentic imagination of what is proper to it, is always, for Keats, startling, novel, original and recognised instantly as true.

These workings of the imagination are in stark contrast to the workings of the intellect, to the processes of 'consequitive reasoning'. The results of intellectual analysis are always there, immobile and available for reference, whereas the originality of the imagination's recognition of its proper pith is perceived as a mystery by the perceptive soul. The moments of the movement coalesce into an elevated moment which springs from them and is new. The 'silent Workings of the imagination' come 'continually on the spirit with a fine suddenness'. It is a thing of 'the elevated Moment'.

Towards the end of this same letter to Bailey, Keats writes that 'nothing startles me beyond the moment' and continues: 'If a Sparrow come before my Window I take part in its existence and pick about the Gravel'.[84] Keats refuses to see imagination as the activity of a dominant passion but rather as its passivity or as a synthesis of both which surprises as unexpected, as original. 'Are we', he asks, 'to be bullied into a certain Philosophy engendered in the whims of an Egotist' who 'can travel to the very bourne of Heaven, and yet want confidence to put down his halfseeing'.[85] This synthesis he later called 'negative capability'.[86]

In his second lecture Hazlitt said of Shakespeare that:

> He was the least of an egotist that it was possible to be. He was nothing in himself; but he was all that others were, or that they could become. He not only had in himself the germs of every faculty and feeling but he could follow them by anticipation, intuitively, into all their conceivable ramifications, through every change of fortune ... He had only to think of anything in order to become that thing, with all the circumstances belonging to it.[87]

Hazlitt replaced *einfühlung*—'empathy'—with something more like *einfüllung*—'a filling up with'. The poet fills himself up with the object of contemplation to such a degree that his own ego is dissolved into the object.

In a letter to his brothers (21 December 1817) Keats recalls a dinner party at the house of Horace Smith. Smith, along with his brother James, had just published their *Rejected Adresses*[88] and had, as a result, been accepted into society as literati. With Horace Smith were 'his two Brothers with Hill and Kingston & one Du Bois', the editor of the *Monthly Mirror*.[89] The conversation was fashionable and witty, the manner of saying something being more important than its substance. In much the same way as etiquette establishes relationships beforehand and then stands between, preventing anything more direct from taking place, wit reduces discourse to the level of expectations.

These wits were not, for Keats, able to demonstrate their individuality because 'they are all alike; their manners are all alike; they all know fashionables; they have a mannerism in their very eating & drinking, in their handling a Decanter'.[90] These mannerisms spilled over into their way of speaking, which was a dominating rather than an attentive listening. Discourse which draws out the unique could never surface in this atmosphere. At dinner that evening Keats said little, not wanting to add to a conversation that was all technical virtuosity and little feeling: 'These men say things which make one start, without making one feel'.[91] As these literati talked it must have struck Keats how sure they were of themselves and how comfortable they seemed in their critical roles. Thomas Hill, the 'literary city drysalter',[92] ending every other statement with the comment 'Sir, I affirm it with all the solemnity of a deathbed utterance, of a sacramental oath'.[93] This difference between wit and discourse is the difference between the neo-classic and Romantic conceptions of poetry. In the one, the speaker thinks he is king, and it is his brilliance that is noticed. He can turn his intellect equally to any subject. He imposes the sharpness of his mind upon the world. In the other, the ego is more ready to subsume itself to its subject. The wit lacks imagination, the ability to put himself at risk. Keats speaks of his 'unimaginative days'—'*Habeus Corpus*'d as we are, out of all wonder, uncertainty and fear;—in these fireside, delicate, gilded days—these days of sickly safety and comfort'.[94] These wits 'talked of Kean and his low company', and Keats comments: 'Would I were with that company instead of yours'.[95] Edmund Kean represents something important for Keats at this time—the actor's ability to exist in his part: 'In Richard he is his sword's dear cousin; in Hamlet his footing is germain to the platform. In Macbeth his eye laughs seige to scorn; in Othello he is welcome to Cyprus. In Timon he is of the palace—of Athens'.[96] Kean refuses the security of 'consequitive reasoning', the safety of wit, and puts himself at risk through imagination. Keats was concerned with this distinction. Wit clarifies and exposes; discourse attends.

After this description of his dinner at the Smiths', Keats speaks of a 'disquisition'[97] he had with Charles Dilke during a walk back to Hampstead from a Christmas pantomime in London. It was as a result of this talk that, as Keats said, 'several things dovetailed in my mind'.[98]

It can be surmised what it was in that conversation which produced this result, because we have a number of other references to Dilke in the letters. For Keats, Dilke was a man who always wanted to know where he stood: 'who cannot feel he has a personal identity unless he has made up his Mind about every thing'.[99] Thus he 'will never come at a truth as long as he lives; because he is always trying at it'.[100] It was Keats reaction against the continual 'reaching after fact and reason' typified by Dilke that decided him as to:

what quality went to form a Man of Achievement especially in
Literature & which Shakespeare possessed so enormously—I mean
Negative Capability, that is when man is capable of being in
uncertainties, Mysteries, doubts, without any irritable reaching after
fact & reason.[101]

Unlike Dilke, whose personal identity depended on his search for a
truth and on satisfying himself as to what it was, the 'poetical
Character', the character 'which Shakespeare possessed so enormously', has no identity of its own, least of all, some special kind of
identity which can be called 'poetic': 'A Poet is the most unpoetical
of any thing in existence; because he has no Identity'. A poet is
'camelion', 'he is continually in for—and filling some other Body'. So,
whereas 'Men and Women who are creatures of impulse are poetical
and have about them some unchangeable attribute, the poet has none,
no identity':[102]

> As to the poetical Character itself ... it is not itself—it has no self—it is
> every thing and nothing—It has no character—it enjoys light and
> shade; it lives in gusto, be it foul or fair, high or low, rich or poor, mean
> or elevated—It has as much delight in conceiving an Iago as an
> Imogen.[103]

Thus, 'Men of Genius are great ... but they have not any
individuality, any determined Character'.[104] This distinction was
talked over by Keats and Richard Woodhouse in their conversations
and recorded in a letter of his to John Taylor immediately after
reading the letter quoted above. Woodhouse wrote:

> I believe him to be right with regard to his own Poetical
> Character—And I perceive clearly the distinction he draws between
> himself & those of the Wordsworth School ... The highest order of
> Poet ... will be able to throw his own soul into any object he sees or
> imagines, so as to see feel be sensible of, & express, all that the object
> itself would see, feel, be sensible of, or express ... he will speak out of
> that object—so that his own self will with the Exception of the
> Mechanical part be 'annihilated' ... it is to the excess of this power
> that I suppose Keats speaks when he says he has no identity—As a
> poet, and when the fit is upon him, this is true.[105]

In Book IV of 'Endymion', and exactly contemporary with the letter to Bailey (22 November) is the description of the Cave of Quietude. These thirty-five lines point forward to all of Keats' later poetry. All his major concerns can be traced back to them. They are too important not to be quoted in full:

> there lies a den,
> Beyond the seeming confines of the space
> Made for the soul to wander in and trace
> Its own existence, of remotest glooms.
> Dark regions are around it, where the tombs
> Of buried griefs the spirit sees, but scarce
> One hour doth linger weeping, for the pierce
> Of new-born woe it feels more inly smart:
> And in these regions many a venom'd dart
> At random flies; they are the proper home
> Of every ill: the man is yet to come
> Who hath not journeyed in this native hell.
> But few have ever felt how calm and well
> Sleep may be had in that deep den of all.
> There anguish does not sting; nor pleasure pall:
> Woe-hurricanes beat ever at the gate,
> Yet all is still within and desolate.
> Beset with painful gusts, within ye hear
> No sound so loud as when on curtain'd bier
> The death-watch tick is stifled. Enter none
> Who strive therefore: on a sudden it is won.
> Just when the sufferer begins to burn,
> Then it is free to him; and from an urn,
> Still fed by melting ice, he takes a draught—
> Young Semele such richness never quaft
> In her maternal longing! Happy gloom!
> Dark Paradise! where pale becomes the bloom
> Of health by due; where silence dreariest
> Is most articulate; where hopes infest;
> Where those eyes are the brightest far that keep
> Their lids shut longest in a dreamless sleep.
> O happy spirit-home! O wondrous soul!
> Pregnant with such a den to save the whole
> In thine own depth. Hail, gentle Carian!

> For, never since thy griefs and woes began,
> Hath thou felt so content: a grievous feud
> Hath led thee to this Cave of Quietude.[106]

What is the 'grievous feud' that led Endymion to the Cave of Quietude? The story of Book IV is of the events leading to the metamorphosis of Endymion's two loves—the Indian Maiden and the Moon Goddess—into one another, into the 'holiness'—wholeness—'of the heart's affections and the truth of Imagination'. Endymion's passion is 'creative of essential Beauty': 'I have the same Idea of all our Passions as of Love they are all in their sublime, creative of essential Beauty'.[107] Two raven horses 'each with large dark blue wings upon his back'[108] carry Endymion and the Indian Maiden 'high as the eagles'[109] and then fall into a deep sleep:

> Upon the spiritless mist have they outspread
> Their ample feathers, are in slumber dead[110]

As these steeds drift across the sky, Endymion, 'the mournful wanderer',[111] dreams that he is in heaven amongst the gods:

> He tries the nerve of Phoebus' golden bow
> . . . .
> Upon his arm he braces Pallas' shield
> And strives in vain to unsettle and wield
> A Jovian thunderbolt[112]

Finally, he sees Diana as 'she rises crescented'.[113] At this moment of recognition of Diana, 'his very goddess',[114] he finds that his dream, what the imagination had seized as beauty, was truth. He 'beheld awake his very dream'.[115] 'The imagination may be compared to Adam's dream—he awoke and found it truth'.[116] Yet, for Keats, this is still 'perplexing'.[117] Like Daedalus:

> who died
> For soaring too audacious in the sun[118]

at the same moment as:

> His heart leapt up as to its rightful throne[119]

he is conscious of:

> the panting side
> Of his delicious lady[120]

—the Indian Maiden. he cannot yet identify the imagination and the heart's affections: they are feuding and irreconcilable opposites—a 'perplexity'.[121] 'All his soul was shook':[122]

> His heart leapt up as to its rightful throne,
> To that fair shadow'd passion puls'd its way—
> Ah, what perplexity! Ah, well a day!
> So fond, so beauteous was his bed-fellow,
> He could not help but kiss her: then he grew
> Awhile forgetful of all beauty save
> Young Phoebe's, golden hair'd; and so 'gan crave
> Forgiveness: yet he turn'd once more to look
> At the sweet sleeper,—all his soul was shook,—
> She press'd his hand in slumber; so once more
> He could not help but kiss her and adore[123]

In the very midst of this feuding of his two passions, of this perplexity of the heart's affections, he demands to know why his heart should be 'wrung / To desperation':[124]

> Is there nought for me,
> Upon the bourne of bliss, but misery?[125]

Endymion is torn between his two loves, failing to see that they are but two aspects of the same and that his misery is caused by his inability to see the whole which is greater than its parts. At the very instant at which the tension becomes insupportable, the negations—the Indian Maiden and Diana—become contraries and dissolve into the whole. Endymion gazes at the Indian Maiden, whose:

> gentle soul
> Hath no revenge in it

and asks himself:

> as it is whole
> In tenderness, would I were whole in love![126]

As he asks the question, he is overtaken by the event. His Selfhood
dissolves, and that which he desires dissolves with it. Even though
Keats is using words here less accurately than he does later, his
description is a masterpiece of psychological observation, and perhaps
something more:

> Her gentle soul
> Hath no revenge in it: as it is whole
> In tenderness, would I were whole in love!
> Can I prize thee, fair maid, all price above,
> Even when I feel as true as innocence?
> I do, I do. What is the soul then? Whence
> Came it? It does no seem my own, and I
> Have no self-passion or identity.
> Some fearful end must be: where, where is it?
> By Nemesis, I see my spirit flit
> Alone about the dark[127]

As his spirit, Self-less, passion-less, flits alone about the dark, the
objects of his love dissolve also. Diana 'bow'd into the heavens her
timid head',[128] and when Endymion turns to his earthly love:

> He saw her body fading gaunt and spare
> In the cold moonshine
> . . . .
> —he was alone[129]

Diana bow'd her head into the heavens, and the Indian Maiden's
steed:

> Dropt hawkwise to the earth[130]

Vanishing as contraries in opposite directions they desert Endymion.
Perceived as oppposites they remained irreconcilable but, beyond the
confines of seeming, where the soul, the Self, tries to trace its own

existence, lies the Cave of Quietude. Woe—hurricanes beat ever at the gate of this den, and outside is nothing but perplexity, feuding and misery—the antagonism of irreconcilable opposites. Redemption lies in the recognition that contraries need one another. As Blake memorably wrote:

> There is a Negation & there is a Contrary
> The Negation must be destroy'd to redeem the Contraries[131]

The whole redeems: the holiness of the heart's affections *is* the truth of imagination. The Cave of Quietude is the den that saves the whole, it is beyond the space in which we seem able to think about existence, the space where negations remain negations and thus unredeemed; unsaved. Griefs are buried as newborn woes strike. This is what man is born to; it is native to him:

> the man has yet to come
> Who hath not journeyed in this native hell[132]

and Keats continues:

> But few have ever felt how calm and well
> Sleep may be had in this deep den of all[133]

These 'few' are saved by becoming 'whole' and are pregnant with such a possibility which cannot be imposed:

> O wondrous soul!
> Pregnant with such a den to save the whole
> In thine own depth[134]

A solution—a dissolution—of negations; a dissolving of negations into one another, is beyond 'consequitive reasoning'. It occurs:

> Just when the sufferer begins to burn[135]

It is a gift:

> Enter none
> Who strive therefore: on a sudden it is won[136]

What is won is the acceptance of opposites:

> Happy gloom!
> Dark paradise! where pale becomes the bloom
> Of health by due; where silence dreariest
> Is most articulate; where hopes infest;
> Where those eyes are the brightest far that keep
> There lids shut longest in a dreamless sleep.[137]

This is a disolution of contraries in which 'all disagreeables evaporate',[138] in which 'pleasure has no show of enticement and pain no unbearable frown',[139] in which 'anguish does not sting; nor pleasure pall'.[140] In this indolent state:

> Pain had no sting, and pleasure's wreath no flower[141]

Here 'Sleep may be had',[142] and the sleep of this den is 'pregnant', its silence is articulate and saves the whole. The soul, now Self-less, has redeemed the contraries and can articulate that redemption. Endymion can now accept that:

> Against his proper glory
> Has my own soul conspired[143]

and:

> had but my footsteps worn
> A path in hell, for ever would I bless
> Horrors which nourish an uneasiness
> For my own sullen conquering.[144]

In the final half of the final book of 'Endymion' Keats brings home this lesson in more concrete terms. Endymion renounces both Diana and the Indian Maiden. He tells the Indian Maiden that she has redeemed him from his dreams of the goddess:

> thou redeemest hast
> My life from too thin breathing: gone and past
> Are cloudy phantasms[145]

But her reply is that she cannot love him:

> I may not be thy love: I am forbidden[146]

She is forbidden also to tell where she is to go:

>   henceforth
> Ask me no more! I may not utter it,
> Nor may I be thy love[147]

Thus Endymion loses both his loves and is again alone. The movement which took him into the Cave of Quietude is repeated, and his two loves, both renounced, now dissolve into one another and are recognised as one—as whole—and therefore holy. He looks at the Indian Maiden and sees that:

>   into her face there came
> Light, as reflected from a silver flame:
> Her long black hair swell'd ampler, in display
> Full golden; in her eyes a brighter day
> Dawn'd blue and full of love. Aye, he beheld
> Phoebe, his passion![148]

3

Silence

I

Criticisms of the 'Ode on a Grecian Urn' usually suggest that Keats is making a comparison between the eternal ideal of art and the impermanence of human existence. The ode, after addressing a series of questions to the urn, makes a seemingly clear statement as to the priority of the ideal over the sensual:

> Heard melodies are sweet, but those unheard
> Are sweeter; therefore[1]

because the ode grants us an artistic vision of that ideal state to which we yearn to escape:

> ye soft pipes, play on;
> Not to the sensual ear, but, more endear'd,
> Pipe to the spirit ditties of no tone.

The ode depicts an ideal love whose passion is eternal, and the dramatic action of the moment both frozen into a permanence which takes us beyond the limitations of thought to a conception of the beautiful and the true. The urn, a representation of the eternal, a 'sylvan historian', will grant its message to others:

> When old age shall this generation waste,
> ... in midst of other woe
> Than ours

The message will be true because it is eternal and absolute, and it will be beautiful because it is caught and held in the perfection of a work of art. The message is that art, the urn, grants us a beautiful conception which is objectively valid over and above the mutability of existence. The urn, by arranging its few facts beautifully, gives us an insight into their truth, which is, by extension, valid for all facts.

Yet this analysis leaves us with a number of puzzles. Much has been made of the structural difficulties of the final two lines and, more especially, of the expression 'Beauty is truth, truth beauty'. Yet these are hardly isolated problems. The rest of the poem also has syntactical difficulties, which for the most part are left unconsidered.

There are, in effect, five sentences in five stanzas. Keats seems reluctant to complete, to close off, what he is saying, as if what he wants to express cannot easily be stated. The sentences themselves are not so much sentences as lists, and in stanzas one and four they are lists of questions. Even the first subject of the poem, the urn itself, is described three times in subject clauses before the appearance of the verb that carries the sentence through:

> Thou still unravish'd bride of quietness,
>   Thou foster-child of silence and slow time,
>   Sylvan historian

Surely the poet's intention here cannot be to help us visualise a particular urn clearly in our mind's eye. Indeed, the details that we are given are, as often as not, couched in questions:

> What leaf-fring'd legend haunts about thy shape
>   Of deities or mortals, or of both,
>   In Tempe or the dales of Arcady?
> What men or gods are these? What maidens loth?
>   What mad pursuit? What struggle to escape?
>   What pipes and timbrels? What wild ecstacy?

Seven questions in six lines and, in effect, one sentence for the whole stanza. The fourth is also a stanza of questions. Excluding question marks (of which, in the first stanza, six are almost superfluous except for emphasis), there are only five full stops in the entire five stanzas.

The problem with the expression 'Beauty is truth, truth, beauty' is that it presents us with an obvious syntactical problem, whereas the rest of the ode can be accepted as more of less valid if 'poetic'. But perhaps these less obvious difficulties should prepare us a little for those last lines. Throughout the ode the reader is left hanging in the air. He is nowhere presented with a clear statement in a logical syntactical form, with a piece of linguistic *terra firma* on which he can stand with security. If the ode is read with care and its 'meaning' not forced into statements in prose, then its ground shifts mercilessly.

The ode is supposed to be a glorification of the eternal beauties of art over the impermanence and corruption of nature:

> Heard melodies are sweet, but those unheard
> Are sweeter

Yet the possibility that Keats intended these words to be taken ironically, to be taken as one more question to be placed against the more structured questions of the ode, is largely ignored. Indeed, the whole structure of the ode is one of an opening up of uncertainties to question. None of these 'statements' are quite what they seem.

In stanzas two and three Keats seems to be drawing idyllic pictures of young lovers enjoying a bliss that is eternal:

> For ever wilt thou love and she be fair

The boughs are 'happy, happy boughs', the melodist is 'happy', the love on the urn is also 'happy':

> More happy love! more happy, happy love!
> For ever warm and still to be enjoy'd,
> For ever panting, and for ever young

In the third stanza Keats uses the word 'happy' six times—perhaps just a little too often. What is it he is presenting here as eternal? Certainly not any of the abstract ideals at which religion and metaphysics usually aim. No, he is describing as ideal and permanent exactly that sensuality which is usually taken to detract from its realisation, most significantly sexual love, but also things which are, to the sensual perception, most impermanent: the first hearing of a new song, spring boughs laden with leaves, and sacrifice. Even then Keats does not simply show as enviable these sensual pleasures, frozen into an eternal moment; rather, the reverse. The picture which the ode grants us is couched in negatives:

> Fair youth, beneath the trees, thou canst not leave
> Thy song, nor ever can those trees be bare;
> Bold lover, never, never canst thou kiss
> ... — yet, do not grieve;

She cannot fade, though thou hast not thy bliss,
. . . .
                    boughs! that cannot shed
Your leaves, nor ever bid the Spring adieu

There are fourteen negatives in three stanzas. Even the sensual esctasy so praised in Keats is not quite what it seems here; although syntactically positive it has an undertow of tragedy:

More happy love! more happy, happy love!
For ever warm and still to be enjoy'd,
For ever panting and for ever young

For ever wilt thou love, and she be fair!

In these lines the very permanence itself seems to be a loss. Indeed, the picture that Keats is painting is, as he says in his last stanza, a 'cold pastoral'.

In the fourth stanza the uncertainty of time and place, of actuality, seems to detract from the relevance of the sacrifice. Neither gods nor mortals can be identified; there is no distance between priest and gods to be bridged by the sacrificial gift. This 'little town … emptied of its folk':

                    for evermore
Will silent be; and not a soul to tell
Why thou aren't desolate, can e'er return.

These three lines at the end of the fourth stanza prepare us for the difficulties of the fifth. Prior to this there is no suggestion that the figures on the urn, let alone the urn itself, speak out; rather, the emphasis is on its inability to speak, its silence. Perhaps all the questioning, all the syntactical muddle, is concentrated here as a pointer towards the final stanza. Perhaps the urn is, above all, 'silent' without a 'soul' to speak.

In this ode it is silence that speaks. The most astonishing feature of the final stanza is not so much the infamous last two lines, which have caused so many problems for the critics, but the fact, almost wholly ignored, that it is silence that speaks them:

> Thou silent form ...
> ....
>   ... shalt remain ...
>   ... a friend to man, to whom thou say'st

One of the most pervasive facets of the ode as a whole is the hush through which we encounter it. The silence which speaks the mysterious and inexplicable statement at the close of the poem is prefigured in the opening:

> Thou still unravish'd bride of quietness,
> Thou foster-child of silence

The urn is both bride and child of silence, a relationship which is both close and committed and yet not quite the normal blood tie, the total and consumated relation, for the bride is 'unravished', the child a 'foster-child'. Silence seems rather to be there ready to fulfil what it promises—a steady gift which is ready as an offer. Also, the ode opens, speaking to the urn: 'Thou still'. The first publication of the ode in *The Annals of the Fine Arts* of 1820 has a comma after the 'still', and this comma has the effect of changing this word from an adverb into an adjective.[2] In this version it does not mean 'as yet' but 'silent', and this is a sense in which Keats frequently uses it. Thus the urn is 'still', 'bride of quietness' and 'foster-child of silence'—a three-fold repetition which must be taken into consideration. This silent urn:

>   canst thus express
>   ... more sweetly than our rhyme

The first thing that the poet speaks is a renunciation of the hardly begun poem in favour of the subject about which it speaks—the urn—which is speechless. The poet renounces language in favour of that which has no language. Yet at the end of the poem it is the urn which 'say'st', which passes on the message over which the critics stumble.

All this is a problem only so long as we refuse to take in what the poet is speaking in the poem and, as we tend to do because of our training, hear only what he speaks *about*. The poet is not so much inviting us to undergo an experience with the urn as an experience with language. The critical approach to the poem has always been a discussion of what the language of the poem is about—an event, the relating of a set of facts. In doing this, language is forced to act merely as a symbol which mediates between the mind of the speaker or writer and the object about which he speaks. Language here cannot bring itself into expression but does exactly the reverse: that is, it holds itself back while we concentrate on what it means.

What the poet invites us to attend to is the Grecian urn. It is the urn that 'say'st' the famous two-line imperative at the close of the ode, and yet the urn is a 'silent form'. When a critic tries, however ingeniously, to explain what these lines mean, he is relying, more or less, on the accepted signification of the words and their syntactical relationships: he is, in effect, explaining what is already understood. The problem, such as it is, lies in the peculiarity of the syntactical relation in which words with otherwise clear significations are placed. When the critic does this, he simply translates a symbol, if in a new and enlightening way. In doing this, as in everyday speech, language remains a set of symbols which we use. We concentrate not on the words themselves but on their meaning. In other words, language holds itself back, and the more clearly we speak, the more inconspicuous language becomes. In this type of situation, we stop thinking for a moment about the meaning we are trying to convey and become conscious of language itself exactly at the moment when language fails us, when we are suddenly unable to call up the word we need. In that moment language brings itself to the fore. Usually when this occurs we look around for another symbol that will do the job and use that to convey our meaning. This is an experience that we all have from time to time when we know what we want to say. But what of the poet who, rather than himself wanting to speak, wants language to speak? In this event everything depends upon whether language grants or withholds the word. If, after attending to it, the word speaks for the poet, then we are given a new signification which, if we attend to it with care, unfolds for us the momentary delay out of which it arose into speech. We can then choose either to concentrate on the new meaning and absorb it—which we tend to do culturally anyway—or to return to its source, to feel for the hiatus out of which it sprang. But the poet recognises this hiatus as the root from which sprang the new growth and its radical signification, which in its turn is there for culture to absorb.

It is this hiatus, this source, which is fundamental, and sometimes to such an extent that the poet is coerced into expressing this itself; that is, into putting into language the experience which language itself compels him to undergo.

It is the 'still' urn, the 'bride of quietness', the 'foster-child of silence' that:

> canst thus express
> ... more sweetly than our rhyme

What is it that silence can do more sweetly than poesy? Keats says 'express'. Ex-press. 'Press' is a word used rarely in Keats' letters; but on three of these occasions the word is important, for he is speaking of the 'poetical Character'. In a letter to Richard Woodhouse (27 October 1818) Keats answers a point raised by Woodhouse as to his opinion of the 'poetical Character'. Keats says of it that it 'is not itself—it has no self—it is in every thing and nothing—It has no character.[3] One of the adjectives he uses to describe the poet is 'camelion'.[4] 'I have', he says, 'no nature. When I am in a room with People ... the identity of every one in the room begins so to press upon me that, I am in a very little time annihilated'.[5] Keats wrote this shortly before the death of his adored brother Tom while nursing him at his bedside. In a letter to Dilke a month earlier he had written:

> I wish I could say Tom was any better. His identity presses upon me so all day that I am obliged to go out—and although I intended to have given some time to study alone, I am obliged to write and plunge into abstract images to ease myself of his countenance, his voice and feebleness—so that I live now in a continual fever—it must be poisonous to life.[6]

It was, indeed, 'poisonous to life'. As we can now conjecture, it was the time spent at Tom's bedside with all the doors and windows closed, breathing in air heavy with tubercle bacilli, that animated the illness which finally killed him. But poisonous to his poetical life it was not. Immediately following this passage, Keats adds 'although I feel well'; indeed, at this time he was composing 'Hyperion'.

For Keats, 'annihilation' is the ground from which poetry springs. The poet, he seems to be saying, should not be a Self—an ego—which stands out over against a world beyond it; a world which is perceived by the poet through the sense organs in a more or less original or striking way through the implementation of fancy, a faculty also learned. This is not Keats' explanation of the 'poetical Character'. He writes:

As to the poetical Character itself . . . it is not itself—It has no self—it is every thing and nothing—it has no character—it enjoys light and shade; it lives in gusto, be it foul or fair, high or low, rich or poor, mean or elevated—It has as much delight in conceiving an Iago as an Imogen . . . A Poet is the most unpoetical of any thing in existence; because he has no Identity—he is continually in for and filling some other Body—The Sun, the Moon, the Sea and Men and Women who are creatures of impulse are poetical and have about them an unchangeable attribute—the poet has none; no identity—he is certainly the most unpoetical of all God's Creatures.[7]

'A poet is the most unpoetical of any thing in existence; because he has no Identity'. 'What shocks the virtuous philosopher, delights the camelion Poet'.[8] It is not the poet who speaks, because the poet as poet is not poetical; he has not about him an unchangeable attribute, for his identity is annihilated:

> if I am ever free from speculating on creations of my own brain, then not myself goes home to myself: but the identity of every one in the room begins so to press upon me that, I am in a very little time annihilated—not only among Men; it would be the same in a Nursery of children.[9]

It is this annihilation of identity that enables the poet to 'plunge into abstract images',[10] 'those abstractions which are my only life',[11] those images which are not the 'seeming sure points of Reasoning'[12] of the 'virtuous philosopher'[13] but the language of the poet. The annihilation of identity and the renunciation of language are co-present. It is the urn that presses in upon the poet, the identity of which he accepts. Yet the urn is 'still', the 'bride of quietness', the 'foster-child of silence'. It is the hiatus in the flow of words that presses in upon the poet in his annihilation of identity, and it is this hiatus, this silence, that expresses itself 'more sweetly than our rhyme', allowing language itself to speak. Is this a paradox? Elsewhere Keats says: 'The Genius of Poetry must work out its own salvation in a man . . . That which is creative must create itself'.[14] In what way can language, the press of silence, create itself and yet leave us with the poem, the ex-press of language? Our clue must lie in the everyday experience of the withholding of language: that it is only when language withholds itself that we can become conscious of it as language; that as language it

presses in upon us as what it *is*, when, for one moment, we stop
thinking about what we are saying and think the saying of it. What is
the mood in which identity is annihilated and language speaks? Keats
calls it indolence.

In Book 4 of 'Endymion' the hero, rising from the dream of his
beloved, the Moon Goddess, finds himself lying beside his earthly
love, the Indian Maiden. Disconcerted by the intertwining of his two
loves and by his treachery to the Moon Goddess, he asks:

>   What is the soul then? Whence
>   Came it? It does not seem my own, and I
>   Have no self passion or identity[15]

This was written as early as 1817 and is a mere thirty-five lines before
the key passage of the 'Cave of Quietude'. Endymion rouses the
winged horses that appear before them and, with the Indian Maiden at
his side, mounts into the heavens. Once more the Moon Goddess
appears. Endymion turns to the Maiden beside him to see if she too has
seen the vision, only to find her fading away to nothing; 'he was alone'.
In this moment of despair and confusion, after suffering the loss of
both his loves, as Keats had lost both his brothers, for whom he had
'an affection "passing the love of women" '[16] his soul enters into the
'Cave of Quietude':

>   Made for the soul to wander in and trace
>   Its own existence

There 'anguish does not sting, nor pleasure pall' and:

>   Sleep may be had ...
>   ....
>   Woe-hurricanes beat ever at the gate,
>   Yet all is still within and desolate[17]

It is in this state of moodlessness that poetry creates itself. It is the
state of indolence, very close to sleep, in which 'pleasure has no show
of enticement and pain no unbearable frown'[18] and in which we arrive
at a 'complete disinterestedness of mind'.[19]

The blissful cloud of summer-indolence
  Benumb'd my eyes; my pulse grew less and less;
Pain had no sting, and pleasure's wreath no flower[20]

It is in this moodless state that three 'figures on a marble urn' appear:[21]

The first was a fair Maid, and Love her name;
  The second was Ambition, pale of cheek,
    And ever watchful with fatigued eye;
The last, whom I love more, the more of blame
  Is heap'd upon her, maiden most unmeek,
    I knew to be my demon Poesy[22]

In this moodlessness of indolence, 'Neither Poesy, nor Ambition, nor Love have any alertness of Countenance'[23] they hold no attractions but rather:

steal away, and leave without a task
My idle days

They faded, and, forsooth! I wanted wings:
  O folly! What is Love! and where is it?
And for that poor Ambition—it springs
  From a man's little heart's short fever-fit;
For Poesy!—no,—she has not a joy,—
  At least for me,—so sweet as drowsy noons,
  And evenings steep'd in honied indolence[24]

Yet this moodlessness of indolence is not creatively negative. It is not a 'nothingness', for the poet continues:[25]

Ripe was the drowsy hour[26]

What is it that the 'drowsy hour' is ripe for but poesy? 'Ripe' is a word which appears at a crucial moment of 'King Lear', where Edgar says to Gloucester:

Men must endure
Their going hence, even as their coming hither:
Ripeness is all[27]

It is in this moodless state of indolence close to sleep, when identity has been annihilated, that poesy creates itself. It is in the 'Cave of Quietude', where the poet is 'ripe' for creation and where:

> silence dreariest
> Is most articulate.[28]

Keats is not saying here that he, the poet, is articulate, but that silence is articulate. It is not through an effort of will on the part of the poet that the poem is created, but through a renunciation of that will and of all others. It is silence, the renunciation of language, that allows the urn to be—to throw itself willynilly into existence—because the poet has renounced his need of it. It is silence that speaks, that is articulate. Silence is ex-pressed in the moodlessness of indolence, when the lack of the word presses in upon the poet.

In the case of the 'Ode on a Grecian Urn',it is the urn that is 'still', the 'bride of quietness' and the 'foster-child of silence'. The poet, in the moodlessness of indolence, has taken on the identity of the urn, annihilating his own. The urn:

> canst ... express
> ... more sweetly than our rhyme

It is the urn, the 'silent form', that 'say'st':

> 'Beauty is truth, truth beauty,'—that is all
> Ye know on earth and all ye need to know.

It is the urn that speaks, that ex-presses from out of the silent hiatus in the sea of language, as the poet in indolence lets the word withhold itself. It is a critical preudo-problem whether the urn speaks the entire two lines, or whether the poet adds the final line and a half as a qualification of the urn's cryptic 'message', or whether the poet addresses these lines to the urn. Indeed, the inverted commas that mark out these words as 'speech', as distinct from the rest of the poem, appear only in the 1820 volume and are missing from the *Annals* as well as from the four extant manuscripts.

II

The silent form that so presses upon the poet:

> dost tease us out of thought
> As doth eternity

Here Keats is using the word 'thought' in a way, common in his day, to mean 'reason', what in his letters he sometimes calls 'consequitive reasoning'[29] and which was at odds with the imagination. In his letter to his brother and sister-in-law (September 1819) Keats accuses Dilke of just such reasoning: 'Dilke will never come at a truth as long as he lives; because he is always trying at it'.[30] He has always to have 'made up his mind about everything'.[31] Even so, Keats considered that rational thought could, combined with other human faculties, be a step on the path towards creativity:

> I compare human life to a large Mansion of Many Apartments ... The first we step into we call the infant of thoughtless Chamber, in which we remain as long as we do not think ... but are at length imperceptibly impelled by the awakening of this thinking principle—within us—we no sooner get into the second Chamber, which I shall call the Chamber of Maiden-Thought, than we become intoxicated with the light and the atmosphere, we see nothing but pleasant wonders, and think of delaying there for ever in delight: However among the effects this breathing is father of is that tremendous one of sharpening one's vision into the heart and nature of Man—of convincing one's nerves that the World is full of Misery and Heartbreak, Pain, Sickness and oppression—whereby This Chamber of Maiden Thought becomes gradually darken'd and at the same time on all sides of it many doors are set open—but all dark[32]

Thought is a stage, and a necessary stage, through which the poet must pass. The danger is that he will get no further, that the manifest attractions of thought will intoxicate him with their 'light and ... atmosphere'. This is more than a simple 'irritable reaching after fact and reason',[33] a need to establish 'certain points and resting places in reasoning',[34] it is one of the human faculties, an important one—intelligence—but working on its own. Creation is not the outcome of the annihilation of intelligence or the annihilation of the world, but of the annihilation of identity.

In his famous letter to his brother and sister-in-law in the spring of 1819, Keats describes the creation of identity:

> This is effected by three grand materials acting the one upon the other for a series of years—These three Materials are the *Intelligence*—the *human heart* . . . and the *World* or *Elemental space* suited for the proper action of *Mind* and *Heart* on each other for the purpose of forming the *Soul* or *Intelligence destined to possess the sense of Identity*.[35]

It is not the imagination alone that makes the poet, nor is it intelligence alone, but the two together, the one acting on the other. This synthesis is achieved through the catalyst of the world, 'a place where the heart must feel and suffer in a thousand diverse ways'. Keats continues: 'The Heart . . . is the Minds Bible, it is the Minds experience, it is the teat from which the Mind or intelligence sucks its identity'[36] For Keats, the soul achieves identity by living in the world. If intelligence refuses to absorb the world of experience, it will limit its thinking to a thinking about, to a Newtonian world which can be only either 'true' or 'false' in a measurable sense—to Coleridge's 'fixities and definites'.[37] The world can only be made real and true through an interaction of it with the Heart and the Intelligence: 'Scenery is fine—but human nature is finer—The Sward is richer for the tread of a real, nervous, english foot—the eagles nest is finer, for the Mountaineer has look'd into it';[38] and 'axioms in philosophy are not axioms until they are proved upon our pulses';[39] and 'Even a Proverb is no proverb until my Life has illustrated it'.[40]

This, for Keats, was more than an existential creed which he had worked out for himself. The axiom was true for him; through his evil star he was closer to it than most. Thought of this type was a real and terrible responsibility from which he dreamed of escaping to an 'eternal',[41] an 'ethereal',[42] a 'sublime',[43] where he could free himself of:

> The weariness, the fever, and the fret
>   Here, where men sit and hear each other groan;
> Where palsy shakes a few, sad, last gray hairs,
>   Where youth grows pale, and spectre-thin, and dies;
>   Where but to think is to be full of sorrow
>   And leaden-eyed despairs[44]

Indeed, for Keats, the experience of these horrors was the prerequisite for entry into the 'eternal':

> 'None can usurp this height' . . .
> 'But those for whom the miseries of the world
> 'Are misery, and will not let them rest[45]

and represented a truth above that understood by Dilke and his like. It is also a truth that reveals itself through silence:

> 'Twas a quiet Eve;
> The rocks were silent—the wide sea did weave
> An untumultuous fringe of silver foam
> Along the flat brown sand. I was at home,
> And should have been most happy—but I saw
> Too far into the sea; where every maw
> The greater on the less feeds evermore:—
> But I saw too distinct into the core
> Of an eternal fierce destruction[46]

This is the eternal which is granted to the poet. Not the Platonic ideal, which is at some remote station in time or place, but the real—the world of misery and joy. The eternal, like language, is constantly around us, but it is easier to rationalise (think about it) than to give it thought (think it). We fail to allow it to reveal its truth.

This promise, which is all around us, has to be accepted. It is the world and our relation to it and the sea of language in which this takes place. This promise we, for the most part, ignore or utilise ignorantly, without thought. It is left to the poet to recognise this promise and not simply to use language to state facts or to rationalise the world into inertia. In 1817 Keats was still struggling with the idea that imagination alone, with or without the philosophic mind, could achieve this, could make the revelation promised by language and the world real:

> have you never been surprised with an old Melody—in a delicious place—by a delicious voice, felt over again your very speculations and surmises at the time it first operated on your soul—do you not, remember forming to yourself the singer's face more beautiful than it was possible and yet with the elevation of the Moment you did not think so[47]

When 'mounted on the Wings of Imagination'[48] it is possible to live for the moment in:

> The real of Beauty, free from that dead hue
> Sickly imagination and sick pride
> Can wan upon it[49]

This is an early speculation of Keats and is put forward in a letter to Bailey (November 1817). It is in part at least the result of his reading of Milton's 'Paradise Lost'. In Book VIII of that text, Adam falls asleep and dreams:

> Abstract as in a transe methought I saw,
> Though sleeping[50]

the creation of woman by God. when he awoke, Eve was standing before him.

> Such as I saw her in my dream[51]

'The Imagination', says Keats, 'may be compared to Adam's dream—he awoke and found it truth'[52]—'whether it existed before or not'.[53] This is, of course, only a speculation, as Keats keeps reminding us. In the 'must be' he is perhaps trying to convince even himself of something about which he is uncertain. But he is not speaking of that kind of certainty. The truth he speculates on here has been given existence by imagination, 'whether it existed before or not'. He continues by suggesting that heaven or the 'eternal', if it exists on the other side of death, must be like this too. This 'truth', he says, will be 'repeated in a finer tone and so repeated',[54] it is 'a Shadow of reality to come'.[55]

Keats is not speculating here that it is the poet who grants existence to things, neither does he speculate that it is the poet who speaks, for he is in the moodlessness of non-identity. No, it is the imagination in the non-mood of indolence that grants existence to things, and it is silence which speaks that existence. If the poet speaks, he will produce only assertions which could then be tested and found to be 'true' or 'false'. Keats is not here interested in that kind of speaking. His concern is the very nature of language, and this nature is exactly *not* to give itself, not to express itself in words, but to withhold itself. The question the poet asks is: Can this withholding speak?. In the same letter Keats says that 'this shadow of reality to come', that to which the indolent and silent imagination grants existence—'whether it existed before or not'—could be a 'vision in the form of youth' and this is, of course, exactly the vision which the poet's imagination grants him in the figures on the Grecian urn. It is 'a vision in the form of youth', it is 'still', the 'bride of quietness', the 'foster-child of silence', and it is this vision, the urn, the 'silent form' that:

> dost tease us out of thought
> As doth eternity.

It is silence that speaks and the 'vision in the form of youth' that speaks.

Contemporary with this letter is the 'Letter to Reynolds', set in rhyming couplets.[56] There are in this letter many reminiscences of the 'Ode on a Grecian Urn' and, although Keats is here in a very different temper, and the letter dates from a full year earlier, the parallels are of some importance. Keats is in one of his lighter moods and the tone is half jocular yet, even here, there is an undercurrent of tragedy. Keats was in Devonshire with Tom who was suffering badly from TB. Twelve days earlier Keats had written to Bailey that 'he has just this moment had a spitting of blood poor fellow',[57] and it was only some six weeks later that he was writing to Reynolds that 'Tom has spit a leetle blood'[58] after which he adds 'but I know—the truth is there is something real in the World'.[59] This 'real in the World' Keats was living, it was being 'proved upon [his] pulses'.[60] He was 'convincing [his] nerves that the World is full of Misery and Heartbreak, Pain, Sickness and oppression'.[61] He was at the point in his poetic life when the 'Chamber of Maiden Thought becomes gradually darken'd and at the same time on all sides of it many doors are set open—but all dark—all leading to dark passages. We see not the ballance of good and evil.[62]

In the 'letter to Reynolds' Keats describes a painting of Claude Lorraine, 'The Enchanted Castle'[63] as he has the 'remembrance' of it in a mood close to sleeping, in which:

> There came before my eyes that wonted thread
> Of Shapes, and Shadows and Remembrances,
> That every other minute vex and please[64]

The painting is:

> Some, Titian colours touch'd into real life[65]

into the 'real of Beauty'[66]—the 'real in the World.'[67]—and there follow
three lines close in feeling to the fourth stanza of the 'Ode on a Grecian
Urn':

> The sacrifice goes on; the Pontiff knife
> Gleams in the sun, the milk-white heifer lows
> The pipes go shrilly, the libation flows

The vision, the remembrance that he wishes to 'shew' to Tom, is not
one of 'eternal fierce destruction'[68] but of joy. As in the 'Chamber of
Maiden Thought', 'on all sides ... many doors are set open', but they
are not now 'all dark—all leading to dark passages':[69]

> The doors all look'd as if they oped themselves,
> The windows as if latch'd by fays & elves
> And from them comes a silver flash of light[70]

and:

> O that our dreamings all of sleep and wake
> Would all their colours from the Sunset take
> From something of material sublime[71]

Keats, as he yearns for Tom's recovery, yearns also for this dream of
joy. Instead he is given:

> the dark void of night. For in the world
> We jostle[72]

where, it seems to Keats, evil is triumphant. He as yet feels too young
to philosophise, and yet recognises that 'consequitive reasoning' can
settle nothing and that he will never win:

> the prize
> High reason, and the lore of good and ill[73]

because:

<blockquote>

                          Things cannot to the will
    Be settled, but[74]

</blockquote>

and here follows a line paralleled in the ode:

<blockquote>

    they tease us out of thought[75]

</blockquote>

Keats surely does not mean here that we have to resign ourselves to the failure of thought, but that thought itself is transfigured into the eternal and *creates* truth—existence—'whether it existed before or not'. Keats speculates on how this may happen in the letter to his brother and sister-in-law of the spring of 1819, which was contemporary with the great Spring Odes. Mind, or high reason, in an alliance with Heart, or imagination, were to be 'proved upon our pulses' and in this way made Soul—'Intelligence destined to possess a sense of identity'. In this way, 'consequitive' thought is transmuted into something quite different: Soul. Whatever 'Soul' is, whatever the highest potential of man is, has to be learned through living, through a sucking in (a pressing in) of experience. For Keats, a man's identity *is* exactly that world in which he lives, and the highest, the most alert, recognition of this is the poetic—the state of 'diligent Indolence'[76] in which the world becomes the poet. These things drive us into the third chamber of the 'Mansion of Many Apartments', a chamber beyond that of 'Maiden Thought', of 'consequitive reasoning'. 'The lore of good and ill' cannot be settled by reason but lies in sublime eternality, 'the real in the World', Adam's dream that he found on waking to be truth. The urn, 'still', the 'bride of quietness', the 'foster-child of silence':

<blockquote>

                          dost tease us out of thought
    As doth eternity

</blockquote>

The renunciation of identity in the moodlessness of indolence is at one with the renunciation of language. The poet renounces all in order to win all:

<blockquote>

    let us not therefore go hurrying about and collecting honey-bee like, buzzing here and there impatiently from a knowledge of what is to be

</blockquote>

aimed at: but let us open our leaves like a flower and be passive and
receptive—budding patiently under the eye of Apollo and taking hints
from every noble insect that favours us with a visit.[77]

Keats was 'led into these thoughts ... by the beauty of the morning
operating on a sense of Idleness'[78] 'The morning' said:

> O fret not after knowledge—I have none,
>   And yet my song comes native with the warmth.
> O fret not after knowledge—I have none,
>   And yet the Evening listens. He who saddens
> At thought of idleness cannot be idle,
> And he's awake who thinks himself asleep.[79]

Adam's dream was 'the real of Beauty' and existed. If, instead of 'an
irritable reaching after fact and reason' beyond the neighbourhood of
our own lives, we attend to that neighbourhood itself with care in
'diligent Indolence', the doors will 'ope themselves' and reveal
existence. It will:

> tease us out of thought
> As doth eternity

Eternity—that creation that creates itself 'whether it existed before or
not'. If we allow silence to speak it says:

> Beauty is truth, truth beauty

This is what the withholding of language speaks, this is what creativity
creates of itself, what grants to the imagination the power to know
what it is, for it:

> is all
> Ye know on earth, and all ye need to know.

It is tempting to treat this saying of the urn as an assertion, two parts
of a statement each held apart from the other by a comma and each an
inversion of the other. In the first, 'beauty' is the subject qualified by
'truth', and in the second, 'truth' is the subject qualified by 'beauty'. In
each case, that which is qualified is not 'higher' or more universal than

that which qualifies it; the object is not descriptive of the subject. Even if we attempt to force it into the qualifying role it might have in everyday syntax, the inversion follows to destroy the meaning we have constructed. Our automatic preconceptions of the structure of language are broken down. A substantive is qualifying another substantive and then being qualified by it. These substantives are themselves the same kinds of abstractions formed by the same kind of grammatical trick as are the ideals of Plato; they are reifications of adjectives—in effect, adjectives prefixed by the definite article,—'the beautiful', 'the true'.

For Keats, they are indeed absolutes, or abstractions, but not in the Platonic sense. The lines:

> Heard melodies are sweet, but those unheard
> Are sweeter

are not a Keatsian updating of Plato and in no way mean that ideal or absolute melodies are truer than the mutable earthly ones that are heard with the 'sensual ear'; rather, the reverse. For Keats, it is exactly the lived experience, the 'proving upon our pulses', 'that schools an Intelligence and makes it a Soul'. It is this Soul, through a renunciation of identity, through a letting of language withhold itself, that prophesies—that utters the word that grants existence to things, 'whether [they] . . . existed before or not'. This very letting of language withhold itself speaks prophetically: the urn 'say'st'. The poet, renouncing the right that is usually taken to be his, grants the right of creativity to create itself. What the urn 'say'st' is not ex-clamation but ex-pression—a letting of truth be. The urn does not speak 'to the sensual ear' but 'to the spirit ditties of no tone'.

Thus, the critical dilemma of exactly who speaks what and to whom, which is left wide open to discussion because of the varieties of punctuation in the various extant manuscripts and printings of the ode, is superfluous. It is, however, interesting to note that both in the earliest known transcript (that of George Keats in the British Library) and the earliest printing (in the *Annals*) there is no colon after 'say'st' and no inverted commas after the saying that the urn 'say'st'.

To say is to prophesy. Letting the word withhold itself prophesies. The withholding of the word allows 'creativity to create itself'. Adam's dream was prophetic, for 'when he awoke he found it truth'. Adam's dream is the eternal, the abstract—not the Platonic ideal but the 'real of Beauty', the 'real in the World', which is the product of the Soul in the moodlessness of 'diligent Indolence'.

'What the imagination seizes as Beauty must be truth'. The poet's renunciation—the letting the word withhold itself—is prophecy, for 'when he awoke he found it truth' 'whether it existed before or not'. Here the word can exist of itself, the poem can exist as poem. The poet's renunciation is not a renunciation of the word but a renunciation of himself to the word; that is to say, an annihilation of identity in favour of the word, a letting the word withhold itself, for 'that which is creative must create itself'.[80] This allows language itself to speak and grants existence to the eternal, the abstract, 'whether it existed before or not'.

This renunciation is prophecy; it grants existence to the word. The Grecian urn of Keats' poem is not some hypothetical, actual vase but the urn of his imagination—his Soul. To know what it *is*, we are not to conceive some hypothetical original but simply to read the poem. In renunciation the word commits itself to existence, to 'the real of Beauty'; for 'what the imagination seizes as Beauty must be truth', 'whether it existed before or not'. The renunciation is a letting the word be, for, after all, we have the poem: 'I have the same idea of all our Passions as of Love that they are in their sublime, creative of essential Beauty'.[81] When 'mounted on the wings of Imagination', 'diligent Indolence' allows 'the real of Beauty' to 'create itself'—to express itself—'whether it existed before or not' or, which is the same thing, allows silence to grant existence to the word. In this moodlessness the eternal—Adam's dream—is seen to be truth: I have not the slightest feel of humility towards ... any thing in existence—but the eternal Being, the Principle of Beauty'.[82] It is the 'eternal Being,' 'the real in the World', the 'real of Beauty' that is truth, 'whether it existed before or not':

I hope I shall never marry. Though the most beautiful Creature were waiting for me at the end of a Journey or a Walk; though the carpet were of Silk, the Curtains of the morning Clouds; the chairs and Sofa stuffed with Cygnet's down; the food Manna, the Wine beyond Claret, the Window opening on Winander mere, I should not feel—or rather my Happiness would not be so fine, as my Solitude is Sublime. Then, instead of what I have described, there is a Sublimity to welcome me home. The roaring of the wind is my wife and the Stars through the Window pane are my Children. The mighty abstract Idea I have of

Beauty in all things stifles the more divided and minute domestic happiness.[83]

Sublimity welcomes the poet home to the 'mighty abstract Idea I have of Beauty in all things'.

4

Truth

Why are a nightingale and a Grecian urn the subjects of these poems? The accepted critical line takes both as examples of perfection: the one natural and free, the other artistic and classical. Both appear to Keats as other-worldly, and both leave the poet here in the world of 'Misery and Heartbreak, Pain, Sickness and oppression'[1] with the message that escape is not possible for him. One does this by singing, the other by saying. In each case the message is the thing itself—the perfection of the eternal—and this eternal is not available to the poet except as a message. The nightingale flies away to sing to coming generations as it has to past ones, leaving the poet alone and forlorn, more conscious of his real existence in the world than he was before. The urn, also, remains through the generations, passing on to mortals its message that 'Beauty is truth'.

For the poet the urn is perfect in a particularly desirable sense, for it:

> canst ... express
> A flowery tale more sweetly than our rhyme[2]

that is, because it is the greater poet. The nightingale sings in 'full-throated ease;'[3] and the poet yearns for a potion:

> That I might drink, and leave the world unseen[4]

What the poet is expressing here is the very thing that he insistently maintains is denied him; that is, the ability to express. What the poet yearns for is to step into the region where he can sing as easily as the nightingale, where he can say as the urn says. But this movement is not possible, at least so long as we think of movement as a going from one point to another, of covering distance. Keats yearns to do this. The ideal world of the urn and the nightingale are profoundly attractive to him, and in each case he does his utmost to place himself in the world for which he yearns:

> O, for a draught of vintage! ...
> ....
> That I might drink, and leave the world unseen,
> And with thee fade away into the forest dim.[5]

The intensity of the poetry takes us up into the eternal perfection of the region, where expression itself becomes perfect—an ideal realisation of the poet's dream.

But this kind of stepping, a movement out of the living world into the world of ideals represented by the nightingale and the urn, is not possible. In the 'Ode to a Nightingale' the bird vanishes, and the poet is left hardly knowing where he is, unclear as to the kind of experience he has written about:

> Was it a vision, or a waking dream?
> ... — Do I wake of sleep?[6]

This is the earlier of the two odes. In the 'Ode on a Grecian Urn' something a little different happens. Here, the poet somehow comes to terms with his vision—the gift that has been granted to him in the moodlessness of indolence—and, unlike in the earlier ode, he does put down what the experience has granted him; it is the urn's message. How, in the second ode, does this happen? Not by way of a stepping out of the world in which he lives but exactly by staying in it. This movement, in which he stays exactly where he already is, is the movement open to the poet, and it is the movement which he takes. To lose himself in the ideal world of the nightingale or the urn would be relatively easy. It is a distance which can be travelled from where he is to a region in which he would rather be. For Keats, the temptation to make this movement is profound. This is evident in the nightingale ode, in which much of the concentration is on the method of accomplishing it, to such a degree that, in imagination at least, the poet does actually make the movement, he is 'already with thee'[7] It is not by the 'draught of vintage'[8] that the poet feels that the movement can be made but by poesia itself:

> I will fly to thee,
> Not charioted by Bacchus and his pards
> But on the viewless wings of Poesy.[9]

For an eternal moment the poet hangs on to the nightingale's song and escapes from the 'Misery and Heartbreak' of his own existence. He sees the world as the nightingale sees it. No longer as that place 'where men sit and hear each other groan'[10] but as a natural Eden, where imagination takes over from sense perception, where the poet:

> Cannot see what flowers are at my feet,
> Nor what soft incense hangs upon the bough[11]

and is in 'embalmed darkness[12]—neither quite alive nor quite dead. He must:

> guess each sweet
> Wherewith the seasonable month endows
> The grass, the thicket, and the fruit-tree wild;
> White hawthorn, and the pastoral eglantine;
> Fast fading violets cover'd up in leaves;
> And mid-May's eldest child,
> The coming musk-rose, full of dewy wine,
> The murmurous haunt of flies on summer eves[13]

Sight and smell have given way to the higher perception of imagination, which 'guesses' at a perfect, idyllic nature, to which Keats returned in the ode 'To Autumn'. But here, the poet, having made the movement, having stepped out of the world of 'Misery and Heartbreak' into the idyllic world of the eternal, cannot maintain his vision and feels reality pulling his feet back to where he started. This is the common experience of the mystic. Still yearning for this perfection, he grasps at the only possible way that the journey, the movement, can be made: through the act of dying. It must be noted that it is not the knowledge of death that makes us what we are, not that acceptance of death which makes us turn to where we already are and recognise it for what it is, but death as an event, a moment, longed for, perfect, painless:

> Now more than ever seems it rich to die
> To cease upon the midnight with no pain[14]

Through this movement we can step into the eternal to a perfection which is the world of the nightingale. Here it is not the horror of death which Keats gives us, not the picture of his beloved brother Tom dying in a world:

> Where palsy shakes a few, sad, last gray hairs,
> Where youth grows pale, and spectre-thin, and dies[15]

It is not death as seen from the world, but dying seen as a moment—a movement—through which mortality passes on to the eternal:

> for many a time
> I have been half in love with easeful Death,
> Call'd him soft names in many a mused rhyme,
> To take into the air my quiet breath;
> Now more than ever seems it rich to die[16]

Even the act of dying has been eternalised and frozen into perfection. And the poet realises, finally, that the movement cannot be made. Beyond death, the nightingale would still be singing, but the poet would hear nothing, would himself be mere earth:

> Still wouldst thou sing, and I have ears in vain—
> To thy high requiem become a sod[17]

No, the poet is still here on earth, still yearning for perfection, and yet he has discovered at least something—that the movement is there to be made, not through dying, not through drink, but through poesy.

The nightingale sings. The poet listens. He recognises that the bird has a message, and through poesy this gift is seen as what it is: a gift. the poet recognises it and yearns for it, but the gift that is granted by the eternal and idyllic the poet himself cannot grasp. It is in its very nature to hold itself back. He makes a movement towards it and it vanishes:

> Past the near meadows, over the still stream,
> Up the hill-side; and now 'tis buried deep.[18]

He considers for just that fatal and fleeting moment how to make the movement, and the movement itself intervenes. By making a movement towards the eternal as an escape from the world of 'Misery and Heartbreak', the distance to be covered itself appears as distance—as what it is—and is recognised as being where it is: between the poet and the gift that holds itself back, that denies itself. Once the distance itself protrudes, it is seen as what it is: as gap between the poet and the gift. In looking, if only for a moment, at the distance itself, the poet must take his eyes off the gift, and when he looks again it is already fading from view.

In the 'Ode on a Grecian Urn', written immediately after the 'Ode to a Nightingale', the poet does not make this mistake. The vision of the figures on the urn denies itself to him and, in denying itself, is renounced. If we listen again to the mode of speaking in these two odes, we notice a significant distinction. In the 'Ode to a Nightingale' the bird sings 'in full-throated ease' and the poet listens.[19] The song of the nightingale is perfect and ideal and at one with its message. The trigger for the poem was a historical event.[20] The urn, on the other hand, never existed. It is the case that there exist certain elements of the poet's subject on various vases of which Keats had seen the designs, as well as in the Elgin Marbles, but no particular urn stimulated the poet's imagination. So, whereas the voice of the nightingale conjured up a vision of the ideal for the poet, the reverse seems to have happened with the urn; that is to say, the urn was conjured up by its message, and perhaps because of this the vision is less steady, more uncertain. Because the message of which the nightingale sings seems, however vaguely, to be somewhere:

> In some melodious plot
> Of beechen green[21]

it is easier for the poet to make manifest the distance which lies between himself and the message and to divert his efforts into ways of overcoming that distance—drink, poetry and death—and, as he does so, to lose sight of what it is of which the nightingale is singing. In the second ode, maybe because the poet is not led to the vision by some voice, he is able to renounce the vision and hear the voice. The urn's message is renounced, the poet refuses to stretch out his hand to receive it, he makes no movement towards it, and it is precisely in this refusal that the distance collapses into itself. The poet stands where he is and, in so doing, allows the message to reveal itself as what it is: as that which denies itself to the poet. But what exactly does this mean?

In the 'Ode to a Nightingale' the bird sings and the poet listens. In the 'Ode on a Grecian Urn' the frieze is silent and the poet accepts that silence. He begins the second stanza with words that could almost be a summary of the nightingale ode:

> Heard melodies are sweet[22]

The nightingale sings its message and the poet, yearning for it, makes a movement towards it. But, in the second ode, he has learned renunciation and can add:

> but those unheard
> Are sweeter[23]

We should be careful not to take this as being an assertion of the priority of the Platonic ideal of melody over the sensual earthly perception of it. Keats here is way beyond any such simplistic analysis. The melodies played by the figures on the urn are unheard, not because they are some kind of eternal, perfect ideal which has to communicate itself to us over some void from another region, but exactly because they are saying—and in our very own language, whose authentic being is already with us but which we refuse to acknowledge. Right at the beginning of the ode, the urn and the figures on it are given to us as 'still', as 'the bride of quietness', as the 'foster-child of silence',[24] and it is these figures—still, quiet, silent—these 'unheard melodies', that 'are sweeter'. The poet, now in the region of language itself, has no need to strain a muscle to reach it. He has to do no more than let it be:

> therefore, ye soft pipes, play on;
> Not to the sensual ear, but, more endear'd,
> Pipe to the spirit ditties of no tone[25]

There is no straining towards this region, because the poet is already in it. There is simply a static acceptance of the gift. Here the quest does not transform itself into a question which draws him away from himself towards an answer which, in its turn, posits further questions. He dwells within the region of the quest itself. The poet asks:

> What ... legend haunts about thy shape
> Of deities and mortals, or of both?[26]

The urn, 'still', the 'bride of quietness', the 'foster-child of silence', has a legend, a story, to tell of deities and mortals, and the poet asks what this legend is. He doesn't tell the story because the saying of it would destroy it as legend, as lay. He asks the urn, which is silent, what legend it holds—what legend dwells with it—accepting that it:

> can ... express
> A flowery tale more sweetly than our rhyme[27]

The rhyme is a heard melody. The legend is silent, an 'unheard melody' and, says the poet, 'sweeter'. This expressing that emanates from silence and is sweeter even than poetry cannot be grasped through interrogation. The thrust of the question demands an answer which would destroy the silence. The poet does not expect expression of this sort—a destruction alike of the silence and the question. He asks the urn about its legend of deities and mortals expecting nothing. He simply dwells within the asking and, by doing so, transforms the question into a quest and, renouncing any movement, stays where he is, allowing the urn to grant him its bequest—to appear to him as what it is—as 'still', as 'bride of quietness', as 'foster-child of silence'.

'Quest' in Old English is 'quethe' and later 'quoth'—a speaking or saying. A bequest is a saying which comes into our region, or a saying which is left to us and is ready for saying in our culture; in fact, a legend. A bequest is received, although we do nothing (by being merely what we are) in some relation to the giver. It is granted us without any striving on our part towards it. Rather than moving on from a question to the region of some possible answer, the bequest of the saying legend allows us to reach what most concerns us: the region where we are already dwelling. In the 'Ode to a Nightingale', the poet has learned how tempting it is to see what he most wants the legend to say and, yearning for it beyond all else, perceives it as something other, as over there, and thus permits the distance between its region and his own to intercede. Through this intercession the regions are seen as distinct, and the poet recognises that he must stay where he is and watch the legend fade away, thus denying himself the say of the legend, the singing of the nightingale.

But in the 'Ode on a Grecian Urn', the legend—the frieze pictured on the vase, which is yearned for by the poet every bit as much as was the message sung by the nightingale—is nonetheless renounced. The poet no longer dreams of ways of reaching out for the region of the legend, as he had for the region of the singing of the bird, but accepts it for what it is—as bequest—as that which must be renounced by staying within the quest which allows it to be what is: to be legend.[28] In the nightingale ode, the bird sings 'in full-throated ease' and the poet longs to:

> leave the world unseen
> And with thee fade away ...

> Fade far away, dissolve, and quite forget
> What thou ... hast never known[29]

In the 'Ode on a Grecian Urn', the poet says nothing of straining after the legend depicted on the vase but, renouncing it, stays where he is, in the region where he dwells.[30] Here there is none of the clear-cut dichotomy of the nightingale ode between the suffering earth and the ideal region of the bird's song. True, the region of the frieze is eternal, frozen, perfect, and this is made more emphatic by the choice of the most impermanent subjects—young love, spring trees, new songs and sacrifice. The melodist is 'happy'. There is:

> More happy love! more happy, happy love!
> For ever warm and still to be enjoy'd,
> For ever panting and for ever young

The lover is assured that:

> She cannot fade ...
> For ever wilt thou love, and she be fair[31]

But, at the very moment of idealising this eternal vision, in the very words of its idealisation, it is renounced. In the reiteration of the 'happy, happy boughs', the 'happy melodist', the 'happy love, more happy, happy love!', the very perfection of the world for which he yearns is touched with doubt. The repetition has an undertow of irony. It is the same throughout. The love is:

> For ever warm and still to be enjoy'd,
> For ever panting, and for ever young

The 'happy melodist' is:

> unwearied,
> For ever piping songs for ever new

and the young lover is assured:

> For ever wilt thou love, and she be fair[32]

The poet 'doth protest too much'. The eternal, the perfect, now incorporates a touch, more than a touch, of the static, the lifeless. The lover:

> Though winning near the goal ...
>   hast not thy bliss

> Fair youth, beneath the trees, thou canst not leave
> Thy song

And the 'happy, happy boughs':

> cannot shed
> Your leaves, nor ever bid the Spring adieu[33]

The eternal, for which the poet yearned, has taken on a great sadness. The assurances to the lover that:

> For ever wilt thou love, and she be fair

and that love will be:

> For ever warm and still to be enjoy'd,
> For ever panting, and for ever young[34]

incorporate a profound lack. The poet accepts that, however perfect and idyllic this vision might at first have seemed, our yearning for it is also a denial of it; an acceptance that, in the very act of desiring what it shows us, we turn our attention away from what and where we are and seek for something other. Keats, by renouncing what he most desires, hears the bequest of the urn. The:

brede
Of marble men and maidens overwrought,
With forest branches and the trodden weed[35]

is a 'silent form':

That leaves a heart high-sorrowful and cloy'd,
A burning forehead, and a parching tongue[36]

—that leaves the poet where and what he is. Yet not what he was. The renunciation of the movement has uncovered himself to himself. The poet now accepts that what the saying legend bequeaths him is silence, and this silence:

dost tease us out of thought
As doth eternity[37]

The silent urn and eternity both 'tease us out of thought'. But this is not to indicate that they leave us thoughtless.

In a poem of a year earlier, the 'Letter to Reynolds', Keats gives us a glimpse of his meaning. He has not yet arrived at the point of thoughtlessness of the 'Ode on a Grecian Urn,' but he uses exactly the same turn of phrase. He begins, as in the 'Ode to a Nightingale,' to dream of some idyllic eternal:

O that our dreamings all of sleep or wake
Would all their colours from the Sunset take:
From something of material sublime,
Rather than shadow our own Soul's daytime
In the dark void of Night.[38]

'Our own Soul's daytime' is shadowed 'in the dark void of Night':

For in the world
We jostle[39]

The 'Misery and Heartbreak' of life are beginning to close in on the young poet. His brother is dying, and he might have had premonitions of his own end. In any event, he is beginning to feel the suffering of the world:

> I saw
> Too far into the sea; where every maw
> The greater on the less feeds evermore:
> But I saw to distinct into the core
> Of an eternal fierce destruction,
> ....
> Still do I that most fierce destruction,
> The Shark at savage prey—the hawk at pounce,
> The gentle Robin, like a pard or ounce,
> Ravening a worm.[40]

Yet without this 'the Hawk would lose his Breakfast of Robins and the Robin his of Worms The Lion must starve as well as the swallow.'[41] The poet recognises that thinking about this will reveal nothing:

> Oh never will the prize,
> High reason, and the lore of good and ill
> Be my award

and he adds:

> Things cannot to the will
> Be settled, but they tease us out of thought[42]

at least the sort of thought that Keats called 'consequitive reasoning'[43] or, in the famous letter to Reynolds of May 1818, 'Maiden-Thought':[44]

I compare human life to a large Mansion of Many Apartments, two of which I can only describe, the doors of the rest being as yet shut upon me—The first we step into we call the infant of thoughtless Chamber, in which we remain as long as we do not think—We remain there a long while, and notwithstanding the doors of the second Chamber remain wide open, showing a bright appearance, we care not to hasten to it; but are at length imperceptibly impelled by the awakening of this thinking principle—within us—we no sooner get into the second Chamber which I shall call the Chamber of Maiden-Thought, than we become intoxicated with the light and the atmosphere, we see nothing but pleasant wonders, and think of delaying there for ever in delight.[45]

But by 1819 Keats had the entry into the third Chamber: 'However among the effects this breathing is father of is that tremendous one of sharpening one's vision into the heart and nature of Man—of convincing one's nerves that the World is full of Misery and Heartbreak, Pain, Sickness and oppression'.[46] And 'still do I that most fierce destruction see'[47] 'whereby This Chamber of Maiden Thought becomes gradually darken'd and at the same time on all sides of it many doors are set open—but all dark—all leading to dark passages'.[48] 'Consequitive reasoning'—'Maiden Thought'—is a stage through which the poet passes, and the passage from it is governed by the fact that the workings of imagination cannot be grasped by 'consequitive reasoning'. Keats asks the question:

> is it that imagination brought
> Beyond its proper bound, yet still confined—
> Lost in a sort of purgatory blind,
> Cannot refer to any standard Law
> Of either earth or heaven?[49]

But the question is rhetorical. No standard law, no 'consequitive reasoning'—'Maiden Thought'—can direct us into the mysteries of the imagination. Those mysteries, here called by Keats, 'things', 'tease us out of thought'. The attempt to grasp what is given by imagination destroys it. The poet must remain within the quest humbly to hear what imagination bequeaths him: 'I have not the slightest feel of humility towards ... any thing in existence,—but the eternal Being, the Principle of Beauty'.[50]

This bequest of the principle of beauty is 'in all things'. 'I have', says the poet, 'lov'd the principle of beauty in all things'[51] Not: the principle of beauty—in all things, but: the principle—of beauty in all things. That is, the poet loved the principle of beauty and that this principle is in all things.[52] In other words, it was only possible for the poet to perceive things truly by perceiving their beauty, and that all things perceived truly were beautiful. He had a 'mighty abstract Idea ... of Beauty in all things'[53] and could say: 'I never can feel certain of any truth but from a clear perception of its Beauty'.[54] He also said: 'The excellence of every Art is in its intensity, capable of making all disagreeables evaporate from their being in close relationship with Beauty & Truth'[55] and 'This pursued through Volumes would perhaps take us no further than this, that with a great poet the sense of Beauty overcomes every other consideration, or rather obliterates all consideration'.[56]

This beauty is the bequest of the silent legend. It is what the silence says. It is the very being of language. The being of what in truth *is* can only gather itself into beauty and bequeath itself when the poet renounces the language of enunciation. The legend is 'a friend to man'.[57] The renunciation is what Keats had earlier called 'negative capability': 'that is when man is capable of being in uncertainties, Mysteries, doubts, without any irritable reaching after fact & reason'.[58] This is the faculty that 'Shakespeare possessed so enormously'.[59] This ability to remain in uncertainties is, for Keats, the quest, the remaining in the region of thought which is not 'consequitive', not an irritable reaching after fact and reason, not speculative. In this state in which the straining after results, the questioning of the world, is suspended, the Self—the identity of the poet—is annihilated. Keats writes: 'As to the poetical Character itself ... it is not itself—it has no self—it is every thing and nothing—It has no character ... A poet is the most unpoetical of any thing in existence; because he has no Identity ... he is certainly the most unpoetical of all God's Creatures'.[60]

For the poet, for the individual with identity—Self, character—poetry is something to be aimed at, striven for. In this state poetry, for Keats, could never be great. For that, the poet must be disinterested, must cease to be poetical, in order to become a poet: 'Men and women who are creatures of impulse are poetical—and have about them some unchangeable attribute—the poet has none—no identity, he is certainly the most unpoetical of all God's Creatures'.[61] The poet must remain within the quest and avoid the questioning of speculation: 'When I am in a room with People if I am ever free from speculating on creations of my own brain, then not myself goes home to myself: but the identity of every one in the room begins so to press upon me that, I am in a very little time annihilated'.[62] The poet must be free from 'speculating on creations of ... [his] own brain', because this is the poetical effort of striving after results, of consciously aiming towards the creation of poetry. For Keats, this is a seeking, a questioning, a movement towards a goal set in advance, a breaking up and scattering of that which is unpoetical—the poet's bequest, that which, if the poet is to have it at all, he must receive as a gift.

In what mood is this gift granted as a bequest? In no mood at all, for any mood must be brought by the poet to his task and thus colour the poem. For Keats, 'that which is creative must create itself'.[63] In this moodlessness of indolence, in this negation of mood 'In this state of effeminacy the fibres of the brain are relaxed in common with the rest of the body, and to such a happy degree that pleasure has no show of enticement and pain no unbearable frown'.[64] He suggests that:

> it is more noble to sit like Jove than to fly like Mercury—let us not therefore go hurrying about and collecting honey-bee like, buzzing here and there impatiently from a knowledge of what is to be arrived at: but let us open our leaves like a flower and be passive and receptive—budding patiently under the eye of Apollo and taking hints from every noble insect that favours us with a visit—sap will be given us for Meat and dew for drink.[65]

In this indolent state in which negative capability is possible, the poet achieves a 'complete disinterestedness of mind'[66] in which the three great aims of Keats' life—'Poetry, Ambition and Love'—lose 'any alertness of countenance as they pass ... by'.[67] 'In this rare instance of the body overpowering the mind',[68] the poet is 'unpoetical'[69] and in 'diligent'[70] passivity renounces the language of poetry, refusing to question language poetically in order that it itself my speak poetry. By remaining in the quest, he is granted the bequest. Keats is quite clear about this. Effort, a striving after poetical language, destroys poetry. The poet receives the language of poetry as a bequest in the indolent negation of mood. The poet's capability is indeed negative: 'That which is creative must create itself'.

In the 'Ode on Indolence', Keats sees the most significant three ideas of his life, the things for which he yearned beyond all others—love, ambition and poetry—but in the indolent negation of mood. This ode was written immediately after the 'Ode on a Grecian Urn' and, significantly, the three figures which represent love, ambition and poetry are seen 'like figures on a marble urn',[71] but in a negation of mood in which the poet fails to recognise them:

> How is it, Shadows! that I know ye not?
> How came ye muffled in so hush a masque?
> Was it a silent deep-disguised plot
> To steal away, and leave without a task
> My idle days?[72]

The figures here are 'silent' and 'muffled' and 'hush', and they risk leaving the poet idle, 'without a task'. But the poet adds immediately:

Ripe was the drowsy hour[73]

Why? Because:

> The blissful cloud of summer-indolence
> Benumb'd my eyes[74]

In this state, the figures are recognised, but only in the moment in which they 'faded',[75] and the poet's immediate response is 'to follow them':

> to follow them I burn'd
> And ached for wings because I knew the three.[76]

But this desire is, at the very moment, renounced. It is an 'irritable reaching after fact and reason',[77] an act of ego or Self aiming at a target, and the poet, in freeing himself of it, remains in 'uncertainties, Mysteries, doubts'.[78] He allows them to fade:

> They faded, and forsooth! I wanted wings[79]

This is not now in the sense of 'ached for wings',[80] but in the sense of lacking them. In this acceptance, in this renunciation of his desire for wings to hurry after the figures, the poet sees them for what they truly are:

> O folly! What is Love! and where is it?
> And for that poor Ambition—It springs
> From a man's little heart's short fever-fit;
> For Poesy!—No,—she has not a joy,—
> At least for me,—so sweet as drowsy noons,
> And evenings steep'd in honied indolence[81]

Indolence is more than poesy, for in indolence poesy is renounced and, after all, we have the poem. Keats now says that the figures can:

> Fade softly from my eyes, and be once more
> In masque-like figures on a dreamy urn[82]

The silent forms of the dreamy urn, seen in a state of indolence, that state in which 'that which is creative must create itself':

> dost tease us out of thought
> As doth eternity.[83]

This negation of mood is like a dream, and in this dream, without any overt questioning by the poet, without any striving towards the creation of an artwork, that which is created creates itself; and the poet, on waking, finds it to be truth. As Adam in Milton's text was given Eve as a gift, so the poet is granted the poem: 'he awoke and found it truth',[84] 'whether it existed before or not'.[85] This is how the imagination operates; it is the test of the 'authenticity of the Imagination':[86] 'I am certain of nothing but of the holiness of the Heart's affections and the truth of Imagination. What the imagination seizes as Beauty must be truth'.[87] The poet's imagination is that which, operating in a state of diligent indolence, allows 'that which is creative to create itself', 'whether it existed before on not'. On waking, the poet finds it to be truth. The urn, 'still', 'foster-child of silence', 'bride of quietness', tells a tale, the saying legend, 'more sweetly than our rhyme', and thus we have the ode.

By not questioning the urn, by renouncing 'consequitive reasoning' in a state of diligent indolence, the poet stays within the quest. What is this legend for the poet that it can create itself? The root of the word 'legend' is the Latin *lego*, meaning 'to bring together', 'to collect', or 'to gather in'. In the word 'legacy', it is the gathering together of a man's value to be handed on as a bequest. In a legend what is bequeathed is that which is gathered as queathe or quoth, that is, as saying. Man, the speaker, can say only because he lives in a legacy of language. The saying as bequest is the legacy of a culture, the very language in which the culture swims. In everyday speaking language is subsumed in its meaning. 'Consequitive reasoning' is a questioning of the world which drives us forward beyond the quest that lies hidden in the questioning and on towards an answer. The very language which makes this possible escapes notice. This experience is the experience of not experiencing language. For language itself to rise up and say, the poet must remain within the quest, within the diligent indolence in which the legend can be itself, be what it really is: a bequest. In everday speaking the men and gods of which the legend speaks are broken up and scattered. To recreate them our enquiry must break them down into units capable of being judged in the process of 'consequitive reasoning'.

The poet, on the other hand, remaining within the quest, allows the legend to gather itself up into what it *is*. The *is* of the saying legend is bequeathed to the poet in silence by holding itself in reserve. In diligent indolence the poet leaves this to happen; the legend bequeaths itself to him within his renunciation of it in Self-annihilation. In knowing this he needs to know nothing else. The legend, in bequeathing itself to the poet—and, through him, to future generations—is a friend to man, because it says the speaking bequest of language without which nothing is. Imagination, in a state of diligent indolence, is authentic—is author of itself—and Keats, speaking of the 'authenticity of the Imagination', says: 'I am certain of nothing but of ... the truth of Imagination. What the imagination seizes as Beauty must be truth—whether it existed before or not'.[88] The imagination is author of itself. In indolence the legend bequeaths itself to the mortal poet, whose very mortality is what touches him closest, and speaks to him of what *is*—the recognition that what *is*, is only in the moment of its dissolving into itself:

> Joy whose hand is ever at his lips
> Bidding adieu[89]

and:

> Beauty cannot keep her lustrous eyes
> Or new Love pine at them beyond tomorrow[90]

In imagination, the legend gathers itself together and seizes beauty, love, ambition, poetry, but as that which, gathering itself up into legend, dissolves into itself. The poet is certain of nothing but of the truth of imagination. The legend is 'of deities or mortals, or of both'[91] The gathering to itself of the legend speaks of the nearness of permanence and impermanence, which is the saying of the *is* that grants that nearness to the poet. For this, the legend is 'a friend to man' and tells him:

> that is all
> Ye know on earth, and all ye need to know.[92]

5'

On Overcoming Milton

I

There exists throughout Keats' life and writings a tension between Milton and Shakespeare which, after a moment of crisis, is resolved in favour of Shakespeare. This tension is not unlike the discourse which Blake carries on between Milton and Jesus. Both Blake and Keats, at a certain transitional point in their creative lives, were fired by the example of Milton, only to discover that his influence was acting as a restriction on their inspiration, a restriction which they had, somehow, to overcome. This overcoming led, in the case of Blake, to Jesus and, in the case of Keats, to Shakespeare.

At a critical moment in his creative life Keats wrote: 'I have but lately stood on my guard against Milton. Life to him would be death to me'.[1] In these words he noted a radical change in his attitude towards the nature of poetic creativity, which meant for Keats a change in his attitude to life. He had overcome one attitude to enter into another. The secret of this change, that which lies at its heart, is Self-annihilation—a recognition that to impose order on the world is to dictate its form and that, by dictating its form, that which is true to the world is lost, or rather, left unfound. If the poet creates a world, then the one that is already there is lost or transformed.

Like Keats, Blake too discovered this to be the case. Like Keats again, the discovery was made through Milton. In 'The Marriage of Heaven and Hell' Blake credits Milton with being on the side of the Devil and thus of the creative energy which for Blake is 'eternal delight'. The key passage is:

> Those who restrain desire, do so because theirs is weak enough to be restrained; and the restrainer or reason usurps its place & governs the unwilling.
>
> And being restrain'd, it by degrees becomes passive, till it is only the shadow of desire.
>
> The history of this is written in Paradise Lost, & the Governor or Reason is call'd Messiah.

And the original Archangel, or possessor of the command of the
heavenly host, is call'd the Devil or Satan, and his children are call'd
Sin & Death.

But in the Book of Job, Milton's Messiah is call'd Satan.

For this history has been adopted by both parties.

It indeed appear'd to Reason as if Desire was cast out; but the
Devil's account is, that the Messiah fell, & formed a heaven of what
he stole from the Abyss.

This is shown in the Gospel, where he prays to the Father to send
the comforter, or Desire, that Reason may have Ideas to build on; the
Jehovah of the Bible being no other than he who dwells in flaming
fire.

Know that after Christ's death, he became Jehovah.

But in Milton, the Father is Destiny, the Son a Ratio of the five
senses, & the Holy-ghost Vacuum!

Note: The reason Milton wrote in fetters when he wrote of Angels
& God, and at liberty when of Devils & Hell, is because he was a true
Poet and of the Devil's party without knowing it.[2]

The history of Milton's epic is the history of the fall of Desire and
the usurpation of its place by Reason. The desire that falls is not
merely physical but the whole human potential of which Blake writes
in the most comprehensive of terms:

The desire of Man being Infinite, the possesion is Infinite & himself
Infinite.
He who sees the Infinite in all things, sees God.[3]

This kind of Desire, like creative Energy, cannot be restricted by
Reason, for Reason truly seen is 'the bound or outward circumference
of Energy';[4] it is exactly the form of creative Energy, the form in which
Blake delights, 'for fire delights in its form'.[5]

False Desire can be restrained but only by a false Reason limited by
Education. True Reason, not thus restricted, subordinates the
apparent restrictions learned by Education—by the bodily perceptions—to its own ends and thus passes beyond them. The one is
included and subsumed in the other, not passed over and left behind,
and because of this, it can always reassert itself. In 'The Marriage of
Heaven and Hell' true Energy, which delights in the form of true
Reason, is seen by Blake as confined and restricted by the 'Ratio',

which is a 'mental deity'[6] abstracted from its objects. This separation of abstract ideas from the objects of which they are the ideas was the work of 'Priesthood'[7] which then 'pronounc'd that the Gods had order'd such things'.[8] 'Thus men forgot that All deities reside in the human breast'.[9] Having once forgotten this vital knowledge, Priesthood could label it blasphemy, attribute it to the Devil and establish the rule of Reason over Energy—of 'good' over 'evil'. But, for Blake, Priesthood is the destroyer of human potential, the denier of the truth that deities are not abstracted 'Nobodaddies'[10] but 'reside in the human breast' and that the Devil's party, which fights against Priesthood, is the keeper of the secret of true creativity.

At this stage in his writing Blake saw Milton as one of the guardians of this secret. The Messiah in Milton's two great epic poems is the Satan of Job, and Milton's Satan is the true Jesus. Blake saw into the heart of Milton and realised that his creativity was freer when he was writing of the Devil: 'The reason Milton wrote in fetters when he wrote of Angels & God, and at liberty when of Devils & Hell, is because he was a true Poet and of the Devil's party without knowing it'.[11] The true Milton, hidden away behind the apparent Milton was creatively more at ease in the company of the Devil's party, which was, at this stage, also Blake's party.

'The Marriage of Heaven and Hell' was written at a moment of supreme confidence, and it is in the nature of such things that this moment cannot last. While it does, there is a perfect fusion of the prophet and the artist; that is, of the holy and its expression in the world. For Blake, however, as we have seen, God is no abstraction living in the skies but 'reside[s] in the human breast' and is recognised by the Identity that has annihilated Self; that is, recognised by the true artist as being himself held within the spell of the holy. In this state of Identity the true artist speaks prophecy. The two are fused together, but only in the moment in which the truth of imagination is recognised. Once this vital moment of recognition is dimmed, that part of the artist which speaks prophecy is dislocated from that part which is artist only, and the magic of the spell in which the Imagination is held together is destroyed. Imagination, which is the recognition of the one part by the other, fades. 'The Divine Arts of Imagination',[12] the ex-pression of Identity, is replaced by the arts of persuasion, the battle to persuade the world to recognise the existence of Imagination. In this way, Imagination is transformed into vindication, and the displaying of 'Naked Beauty'[13] which is true and immediate becomes instead a mediation of the Imagination. This is only possible in terms other than its own: in terms of symbolism, theology, metaphysics and mysticism, which are the clothes of beauty and, as such, hide its nakedness. The great prophetic books for the most part are not prophecy in Blake's sense of the ex-pression of Imagination—of letting Imagination stand where it is—but works of gnosis, of mystical exposition.

In this error of Blake's, and later of Keats', lies the greatest peril for the poet, for in the process of vindicating Imagination, Imagination itself, the 'Naked Beauty', moves into the play of this vindication. The poet is forced, paradoxically, by the very strength of his feeling for the truth that he wishes to display, to identify Imagination with its display. In this vindication, the ex-pression of Imagination becomes a mere display, and Blake's art becomes for him the only art. The poet's Selfhood has taken over from his Identity, which is the very annihilation of Selfhood.

Blake realised what was happening, that the Selfhood had reasserted itself, and he recognised also that his hero Milton was riddled with the same error and that this very error was the greatest peril for the creative Imagination. But Blake came to see something more in this error: that the poet's recognition of this peril is itself the essential clue by which he can be saved, saved not from it but by it. The immediacy of the vision granted by Imagination had been replaced by its vindication of a world which could not accept it. Looking for a cause for the necessity of any vindication of the Imagination, he had picked on Reason (*Urizen*) and accused it of subverting the freedom of creative Imagination. It was Reason that was mediating, putting into a mystical or symbolic framework, the immediacy of the Imagination and not simply existing as its natural form. A duality of Imagination versus Reason had taken the place of the unitary experience which Imagination is, and this duality, which is constantly warring with itself, springs from the Selfhood of the artist.

Reason had appeared unregenerate to Blake, exactly because he himself had been unregenerate. He saw that his own Selfhood had interposed itself between vision and visionary; or rather, was that duality of vision and visionary which allows them to war with each other. This duality at war with itself is the greatest peril for the poet. It is also what saves him from the peril. Lying at the very core of a work which is mere vindication is the possibility of letting Imagination stand where it is; that is, of recognising that the duality is itself that

Selfhood that has to be annihilated. Within the struggle between Reason and Energy, at its very centre, lies the recognition that both are elements of Selfhood that have to be annihilated in order that a regeneration of Identity, of Imagination, can take place. Yet, in this recognition, the poet does not finally overcome the duality and thus end the struggle. That struggle itself is his creativity, or regeneration is Imagination. The regeneration of Identity from Selfhood through the annihilation of Self is the collapsing into each other of the warring elements of Selfhood: Reason and Energy. The identity of their common ground—of the ground from which they spring—of the intimacy without which no struggle can take place, is itself the poet's Identity.[14] Thus regeneration is a constant and never-ending struggle and the poet's high responsibility is to live within it and uncover the hidden moment in which they touch each other and are regenerated.

To put this another way: in 'The Marriage of Heaven and Hell' Blake had taken the warring of Energy and Reason to be the struggle of the Self against the not-Self, a conflict which could only be resolved by the annihilation of Reason and the victory of Energy, the poetic vision. Later, he came to see that this struggle takes place within the Self—a struggle of the Self with the not-Self. Blake, seeing this as the poet's struggle with himself, had to accept that the poet who allowed this struggle to dominate was totally absorbed by his own Selfhood. Negation is divided against Negation. Neither can accept any principle beyond itself and each battles to dominate and exclude the other. A Self divided against itself is the form of Selfhood. But from within the dislocation which this division represents for the poet springs the Saviour, in Blake's vision, Jesus himself. Satan, the hermaphrodite, dualistic, Selfhood at war with itself stands now in a new struggle over against Jesus. Jesus, divine Identity, springs out of the struggle within the duality of Self by the recognition in each Negation that it, itself, is the cause of what is hateful in the other. In this way, each Negation is transformed and becomes a Contrary. Contraries do not exclude each other. They need each other. They resolve into each other's field of gravity. They circle in each other's spell. Acceptance of the interdependance of the two permits of their being regenerated, for:

Without Contraries is no progression[15]

Art is Self-annihilation; it is the collapsing into each other of the Contraries; it is the regeneration, the eternal recurrence, of the struggle without which Self-annihilation, creation, cannot occur. Imagination is Self-annihilation. The moment in which Imagination speaks occurs as if in a dream and is only recognised as Imagination on waking. It seems, indeed, to take place outside time Blake writes:

> Every Time less than a pulsation of the artery
> Is equal in its Period & value to Six Thousand Years,
> For in this Period the Poet's Work is Done, and all the Great
> Events of Time start forth & are conceiv'd in such a Period,
> Within a Moment, a Pulsation of the Artery.[16]

Or, as Keats says:

> He awoke and found it truth[17]

That which saves the poet from the peril of Self, which generates its own Negation, is the Saviour, Jesus. The Identity dwells with the Saviour in the miraculous spell of regeneration. In this regeneration lies the poetic work which is Prophecy. The collapsing into each other of the Contraries is Imagination, the immediacy of Self-annihilation. In this eternal moment Prophecy speaks; it is 'a Moment in each Day that Satan cannot find'[18] and lies outside the six thousand years of human vegetative generation. This is the:

> Void Outside of Existence, which if enter'd into
> Becomes a Womb[19]

—the womb in which Inspiration is born, the womb of language, in which the poet goes to 'Eternal Death'[20] which is spiritual resurrection:

> by Self-annihilation back returning
> To life Eternal[21]

which is the Imagination, the potential of each Self lost in the world of generation:

> The Imagination is not a State; it is the Human Existence itself[22]

for:

God only Acts & Is, in existing beings or Men[23]

In travelling this path of eternal regeneration, Blake had identified himself with Milton. As early as 'The Marriage of Heaven and Hell', Blake had seen that Milton had made Satan the real poetic hero of his two epics. Milton's creative Energy was more inspired when writing of Devils and Hell than of Angels and God, because 'he was of the Devil's party without knowing it'.[24] Although apparently siding with the power of Reason, his real allegiance lay with the Eternal Delight of Energy. In the regeneration of Milton's Satan, Blake had found the ·most personal way of expressing his poetic knowledge at the time of the 'Marriage'. For Blake, Milton's Satan was Messiah, the Saviour; and Milton's Jehovah was the Devil. Heaven was seen in Hell and Hell in Heaven. Thus transposed, they could come to a recognition of each other and a marriage take place.

But by the time of the composition of 'Milton', Blake had travelled some way further along the path of regeneration. The marriage of Heaven and Hell, he could now see, was nothing more than the marriage of one Self to another Self, each of which was at war with the other, and thus each of which was in Hell. Not only was Milton's Jehovah the Satan of the Book of Job, but Milton's Satan was that Satan also.

Blake, inevitably, now called on Milton himself to speak this new knowledge. Blake, identifying himself with Milton, had to accept two things. First, that in the marriage of Heaven and Hell, of Energy and Reason, he had been his own Satan—a truth which he had unconsciously known himself. Secondly, that Satan was his own Selfhood, one which must be annihilated in order to overcome the Negations. To overcome this struggle between Energy and Reason, Jehovah and Satan, Blake/Milton must come to know his own hermaphrodite duality.[25]

At the opening of 'Milton' the poet dwells in Eternity while his Emanation, the six-fold Miltonic female (his three wives and three daughters) and his Spectre (Satan) dwell in the world of Memory, of generation:

What do I here before the Judgement? Without my Emanation?
With the daughters of memory & not with the daughters of
    inspiration?[26]

He must go down to the world of Memory, so as to be united with his Spectre and thus also with his Emanation:

> I will go down to Self-annihilation and eternal death,
> Lest the Last Judgement come & find me unannihilate
> And I be seiz'd & giv'n into the hands of my own Selfhood[27]

He goes down into the world of Memory in the hope of:

> by Self-annihilation back returning
> To life Eternal[28]

In this way, life Eternal, the immediate, 'a Pulsation of the Artery',[29] is uncovered by the willing annihilation of Self, which can only occur within the play of the Contraries. By this Self-annihilation Blake/Milton returns to life Eternal. As the garment of the world of Memory falls away, it reveals the Saviour who dwells always in Eternity, because he has no Emanation or Spectre to haunt him. In the loving acceptance of Self-annihilation, within the struggling interplay—the spell of the Contraries—the Eternal Moment, is touched and Prophecy is possible. The poet who, even for an instant, claims the power to speak, who claims the power over the prophetic word, annihilates the power of the word itself to speak prophetically and show itself from within the struggle. Here are Negations and Contraries. But:

> The Negations must be destroy'd to redeem the Contraries[30]

With the struggle of the contraries the world collapses into the Identity who has annihilated his Selfhood. She:

> fled into the depths
> Of Milton's Shadow, as a Dove upon the stormy Sea[31]

and Prophecy is freed to show itself. Thus Milton says that:

> To bathe in the Waters of Life, to wash off the Not Human,
> I come in Self-annihilation & the grandeur of Inspiration[32]

This Inspiration speaks itself within the Eternal Moment and is seen, on waking, to be truth, 'whether it existed before or not'.[33] This is the very nature of Prophecy. When the Bard is asked:

> Where hadst thou this terrible Song?

he replies:

> 'I am inspired! I know it is Truth! for I Sing
> According to the inspiration of the Poetic Genius
> Who is the eternal all-protecting Divine Humanity'[34]

II

In its relationship to Milton, the history of Keats' poetic inspiration closely follows Blake's except, perhaps, in one particular respect. Whereas in Blake, Jesus' presence is hardly felt until the supremacy of Milton has been overcome, in Keats, Shakespeare's presence is always there. Keats hardly speaks about poetry without making some kind of reference, however oblique, to Shakespeare. Even at that critical point in his life when Milton rules supreme, Shakespeare is there knocking at the door. Milton displaces him for a time, but it is only for a time.[35]

On 23 January 1818 Keats wrote two letters, one to Benjamin Bailey and one to his brothers, George and Thomas. In these letters Milton and Shakespeare appear side by side. At just this time, on Tuesday mornings in January and early February, Keats was attending Hazlitt's lectures on the English poets. He says of the second of these on Chaucer and Spencer that he 'went last Tuesday, an hour too late, to Hazlitt's Lecture on poetry, got there just as they were coming out'.[36] If he attended the others on time, he would have heard the third, on Shakespeare and Milton, the following Tuesday, the (27 January); that is, four days after the date of these letters. It is interesting that, even at this early stage, the distinction between these two poets noted by Keats should be paralleled in Hazlitt's lectures a few days later.

Hazlitt put Shakespeare above all other poets and compares him to Milton in terms of ego. Shakespeare's ego dissolves into the world about him, permitting the world to take over. It is, therefore, universal. Milton's ego, on the other hand, is always present and has a tendency to impress itself upon the world. Shakespeare's world creates his art; Milton's art creates his world. By December 1817, Keats had defined this quality 'which Shakespeare possessed so enormously' under the heading of 'Negative Capability'.[37] This way of describing Shakespeare's creative nature was an extension of the concept of sympathy, which was itself derived from the German idea of empathy—*einfühlung*—which, in its turn, was one of the basic tenets of English Romantic criticism. Although more often related to ethics than aesthetics, it did assume that the imagination could grasp the truth of an object it was contemplating by a kind of immediate intuition—a process of which the rational mind was incapable. Keats described it as that state of mind in which 'man is capable of being in uncertainties, Mysteries, doubts, without any irritable reaching after fact and reason'.[38] The poet is he who is able to accept the secret behind appearances and let it remain what it is, veiled from view and secret. The ego which assaults the world in search of substantive evidence, of proof, cannot let the secret be as it is. It has to read it in terms of its enquiry. The world it finds is seen through spectacles tinted with the colours of method. The man who possesses negative capability, on the other hand, subsumes his ego in the world, allowing its mysteries to remain veiled. Hazlitt says, as does Keats, that Shakespeare possesses this quality:

> The striking peculiarity of Shakespeare's mind was its generic quality, its power of communication with all other minds—so that it contained a universe of thought and feeling within itself, and had no one particular bias, or exclusive excellence more than another. He was just like any other man, but that he was like all other men. He was the least of an egotist that it was possible to be. He was nothing in himself; but he was all that others were, or that they could become ... he had only to think of any thing in order to become that thing.[39]

Shakespeare has undercut the epistemological problem over which the philosophers agonise: he has no ego over against the world. For him, the distinction between ego and world is not a distance which has to be bridged. He annihilates his ego and becomes his world: 'When he conceived of a character, whether real or imaginary, he not only entered into all its thoughts and feelings but seemed instantly ... to be surrounded by all the same objects ... the same local, outward and unforseen accidents which would occur in reality'.[40] The world gives itself to Shakespeare in whose plays we have the world. 'The thing happens in a play as it might happen in fact':[41] 'Each of his characters is as much itself and as absolutely independent of the rest as of the author as if they were living persons, not fictions of the mind'.[42] This, for Hazlitt, is what distinguishes Shakespeare from Milton. He writes: 'The passion in Shakespeare ... is not of some one habitual feeling or sentiment preying upon itself, growing out of itself, and moulding everything to itself'.[43] But the passion in Milton is of just this kind. Where Shakespeare's passion is 'passion modified by passion',[44] Milton's is passion modified by contemplation. He 'takes the imaginative part of passion—that which remains after the event, which the mind reposes on when all is over, which looks upon circumstances from the remotest elevation of thought and fancy, and abstracts them from the world of action to that of contemplation'.[45] It is epic rather than dramatic. Milton had a reason for writing, and with this objective he organised the world artistically to fit his purposes: 'He thought of nobler forms and nobler things than those he found around him. He lived apart in the solitude of the own thoughts carefully excluding from his mind whatever might distract its purposes or alloy its purity, or damp its zeal'.[46] Hazlitt realized that because Milton wrote epics and with a purpose, he 'always labours':[47] In Milton there is always an appearance of effort ... the power of his mind is always stamped on every line'.[48]

In the letters which Keats wrote on 23 January, we can see that his reactions to Shakespeare and Milton were running along the same lines as Hazlitt's. He includes in these letter two poems, the first after he had been surprised 'with a real authenticated lock of Milton's hair'[49] and the other 'On sitting down to "King Lear" once again'.[50] The distinction between Keats' reactions to these two poets, each in his own way so important to him, is transparent. Keats' own empathy is at work. In the lines on Milton he retains a calm and calculated distance, a 'recollection in tranquility' which, in both metre and feeling, is not unlike Wordsworth's:

> Chief of organic numbers!
>   Old Scholar of the Spheres!
> Thy spirit never slumbers,
>   But rolls about our ears,
> For ever, and for ever![51]

Here, Keats addresses a spiritual eternal, a poet who, as Hazlitt puts it, 'seized the pen with a hand just warm from the touch of the ark of faith'.[52] Milton's achievement is so other-worldly that the only way to express praise is to offer sacrifice, and even that is mad:

> O what mad endeavour
> Worketh he,
> Who to thy sacred and ennobled hearse
> Would offer a burnt sacrifice of verse
> And melody
> . . . .
> When every childish fashion
> Has vanish'd from my rhyme
> Will I, grey-gone in passion,
> Leave to an after-time
> Hymning and harmony
> Of thee[53]

thus, only after he has excorcised from his verse all the natural childlike intensity, will he be able to offer his sacrifice in rhyme to Milton.

The lines to Shakespeare are the polar opposite of the above. The calm tone of distant admiration is gone:

> O golden tongued Romance, with serene lute!
> Fair plumed Syren, Queen of far-away!
> Leave melodizing on this wintry day,
> Shut up thine olden pages, and be mute:
> Adieu! for, once again, the fierce dispute
> Betwixt damnation and impassion'd clay
> Must I burn through; once more humbly assay
> The bitter-sweet of this Shakespearian fruit.[54]

The poet bids farewell to Romances with their unruffled vision of beauty: 'Romance, with serene lute ... Queen of far-away'. Here, in *King Lear*, is something of a quite different order:

> the fierce dispute
> Betwixt damnation and impassion'd clay
> Must I burn through

Reading *King Lear* is like going through an agony, like being burnt in
the flames of suffering undergone by Lear and Gloucester and, like
them, being transformed. Keats begs, before reading the play:

> Let me not wander in barren dream,
> But, when I am consumed in the fire
> Give me new Phoenix wings to fly at my desire.[55]

Two things distinguish this sonnet from the lines on Milton. The
first is its intensity. As we read, we feel the strength of emotion which
the poet expects to suffer and the intensity of the expectation itself.
The second, which follows inevitably from the first, lies in the quality
of the experience. In the lines on Milton, Keats is praising a kind of
verse in which the reader is left little room for emotional manoeuvre.
The experience has been designed for him in advance. The impress of
the poet's mind has organised his world and reduced the reader's
potential for interpretation. In the lines on Shakespeare,
miraculously, the world is simply itself, and the reader's responsibility
for interpretation is his alone; he seeks the poet's cooperation in vain.
The whole is no longer organised into a pattern. The ego of a powerful
mind has not set its impress on the world and drawn us along to think
with it, to think in its way. In the world of *King Lear* the reader is left to
suffer the same agonies as the sufferers; the poet's subsumption of ego
permits this. He doesn't stand in the way of this suffering world and
interpret it for us; the world itself speaks.

This movement is present in the Spring Odes. Here, the 'egotistical
sublime'[56] is set aside, the Self annihilated and truth itself allowed
utterance, 'whether it existed before or not'.[57] The Miltonic ego which
surfaces in the 'Ode to a Nightingale' is recognised as such and, in the
'Ode on a Grecian Urn', renounced. No ego making use of language
'composed' this ode. Here, Keats' imagination was not operating
consciously in this way. On the contrary: 'The Imagination may be
compared to Adam's dream—he awoke and found it truth'.[58] The
renunciation of Self in the moodlessness of indolence is at one and the
same time the renunciation of language and in this renunciation the
poet is granted the poem—'the eternal Being',[59] 'the real of Beauty'.[60]

But Keats went far beyond this, and he did it with the aid of Milton.
Between mid-April 1819, immediately after the period of the Spring
Odes, and the September of that year, he came to deny the poetic
knowledge through which those odes came into being and then to

rediscover it at a higher level. This process involved, for Keats, a
determination to accept the ideas which he saw reflected in Milton's
verse and then, finally, to overcome them when he came to recognise
the ruinous effect that they were having on his life and poetry.

Having completed the odes, Keats had to face the pressing problem
of earning a living. He had come to the end of his meagre resources and
was discovering the need to 'stand upon some vantage ground and
begin to fight'.[61] By June, his financial affairs were in a very bad state.
His guardian, Abbey, informed him that Mrs Midgely Jennings, his
aunt, was making ready to file another petition against the estate,
which, said Abbey, would put him 'very undeservedly in the wrong
box'.[62] At the time, Abbey told Keats, without any grounds
whatsoever as it now appears, that the monies due to Tom from his
grandmother and for which he had been hoping, should now be held in
trust until Fanny came of age. On 17 June, suppressing his pride,
Keats wrote to Haydon: 'I was the day before yesterday much in want
of Money: but some news I had yesterday'[63]—which concerned the bill
in chancery against the estate—'has driven me into necessity'.[64] and he
pleads: 'Do borrow or beg some how what you can for me'.[65] Again, on
the same day, he says to his sister that he has 'written this morning to
several people to whom I have lent money, requesting repayment',[66]
and he apologises that he is unable to visit her as he 'cannot afford to
spend money by Coachire'[67]—which can have only been a matter of a
few pence. The situation was very serious. On 31 May he wrote to Miss
Jeffreys: 'My Brother George always stood between me and any
dealings with the World—Now I find I must buffet it'.[68]

To qualify as a surgeon in Edinburgh was out of the question as it
would have cost money before making any. This left Keats with two
alternatives, which he mentions in the letter of 31 May: 'I have the
choice as it were of two Poisons ... the one is voyaging to and from
India for a few years; the other is leading a fevrous life alone with
Poetry'.[69] He had already virtually rejected the first of these and
admits immediately that 'the latter will suit me best'.[70] He begs Miss
Jeffrey to ask her mother to 'Enquire in the Villages round
Teignmouth if there is any Lodging commodious for its cheapness'[71]
and to let him know 'where it is and what price'[72]

This settling down to write poetry was possible because his friend
Charles Brown had agreed to loan him enough money to do so. The
idea was for Keats to compose another volume of poetry and also to
flesh out a scenario of Brown's for a play, 'Otho the Great', which they

had hopes of Edmund Kean, the great actor-manager, putting on at the Drury Lane Theatre. That Keats should have agreed to this is not so surprising. Brown had already had a play staged at Drury Lane and had made some £300 at the venture, and Keats' newly avowed aim in writing was to earn a living.

The financial straights in which he found himself were bad enough in themselves; but worse than that, they made marriage to Fanny out of the question, and it was this above all else that was preying on his mind. In order to make money, he must calm his passions for Fanny, leave Hampstead and write: 'I am going to try the Press once more and to that end shall retire to live cheaply in the country and compose myself and verses as well as I can'.[73] In order to compose himself, he needed to put his love for Fanny out of his mind. This was clearly the advice that Brown was pressing upon him, with little thought as to the effect it might be having. Brown was a realist and believed, in his own way, that Keats' passion for Fanny was detrimental to their project of making money by writing. Keats also, for the time being at least, accepted Brown's advice; but the paradox involved in his attempt to forget Fanny was always close to the surface, and eventually had to come up for air. Yet the main reason for his writing for money in the first place was to enable him to marry Fanny. In logic, the means might justify the end, but poetically the process was an unnatural one. As Keats had earlier said: 'If Poetry comes not as naturally as the Leaves to a tree it had better not come at all'.[74] For poetry to come naturally to Keats, it had to come through Self-annihilation in the moodlessness of diligent Indolence. Only then could the Imagination seize hold of the Identity and language speak, so that, on waking, the poet could find it truth. Only when the great conscious aims of life—in Keats' case, love, ambition and poetry—had been subsumed by Indolence could this happen. In the 'Ode on Indolence' Keats writes:

> So, ye Three Ghosts, adieu! Ye cannot raise
> My head cool-bedded in the flowery grass;
> For I would not be dieted with praise,
> A pet-lamb in a sentimental farce![75]

He tells the three shadows:

> Fade softly from my eyes, and be once more
> In masque-like figures on a dreamy urn[76]

In this renunciation of love, ambition and poetry lay the hidden secret of their attainment, and it was exactly this vital renunciation which he was now being denied. He gave up the Indolence which was so precious to his creative life and instead took up Energy, its polar opposite. This decision makes its appearance for the first time in a letter to Miss Jeffrey (31 May). He writes: 'I must choose between despair & Energy—I choose the latter'. A little earlier in the same letter he says: 'Yes, I would rather conquer my indolence and strain my nerves at some grand Poem'.[78]

The impression given by Keats in these letters is that he was forcing himself against the grain. He didn't really want to write, but he felt that he had to. The comparison between these letters and the one to Haydon of 8 March is transparent: 'I have come to this resolution never to write for the sake of writing, or making a poem ... with respect to my livelihood I will not write for it, for I will not mix with that most vulgar of all crowds the literary'.[79] Yet now he was steeling himself to do just this—to write for his livelihood—and this approach to poetry was a major trial for him and, above all, unnatural.

On 8 July he writes to Fanny: 'I am at the diligent use of my faculties here. I do not pass a day without sprawling some blank verse or tagging some rhymes'.[80] To Reynolds, three days later, he writes: 'I have great hopes of success, because I make use of my Judgement more deliberately than I yet have done'.[81] The strangeness of all this comes out later in the same letter:

> I have of late been moulting: not for fresh feathers & wings: they are gone, and in their stead I hope to have a pair of patient sublunary legs. I have altered, not from a Chrysalis into a butterfly, but the Contrary ... The first time I sat down to write, I could scarcely believe in the necessity of so doing. It struck me as a great oddity.[82]

By this conscious and poetically unnatural act he 'set [his] Mind at work'[83] and turned away from his better instincts. It is this betrayal that governed all the creative period that began early in June. He did, indeed, set his mind to work with the most prodigious energy. On 11 July he was writing to Reynolds: 'You will be glad to hear ... how diligent I have been, & am being. I have finish'd the Act and ... have proceeded pretty well with Lamia'.[84] On 14 August to Bailey:

> Within these two Months I have written 1500 Lines ... I have written

two tales, one from Boccacio call'd the Pot of Basil; and another call'd Saint Agnes Eve ... and a third call'd Lamia—half finished—I have also been writing parts of my Hyperion and completed 4 Acts of a Tragedy.[85]

During the two months of July and August Keats wrote 'Lamia', the revision of 'Hyperion' and the whole of 'Otho the Great'. This enormous quantity of words he was forcing out of himself against the current of his natural inclinations. At the same time he was denying his love for Fanny, also against the current of his natural inclinations. The two movements ran in parallel. Keats was forcing out words in order to make money so that he could marry Fanny; but to do this, he had to conquer his indolence—a poetically unnatural act for him—and to do this, he had to force himself to forget Fanny. This dual strain tells on him. He yearns to be with her while, in the very same moment, forcing himself to deny her and remain at a distance and write. On 1 July he tells her:

I will never return to London if my Fate does not turn up Pam or at least a Court-Card. Though I could centre my Happiness in you, I cannot expect to engross your heart so entirely—indeed if I thought you felt as much for me as I do for you at this moment I do not think I could restrain myself from seeing you again tomorrow for the delight of one embrace. But no—I must live upon hope and Chance. In case of the worst that can happen, I shall still love you—but what hatred shall I have for another![86]

And on 16 July he writes:

When I have to take my candle and retire to a lonely room, without the thought as I fall asleep, of seeing you tomorrow morning? or the next day, or the next—it takes on the appearance of impossibility and eternity ... [and yet] I should not like to be so near you as London without being continually with you: after having once kissed you Sweet I would rather be here alone at my task than in the bustle and hateful literary chitchat.[87]

By the 25 July the tension between his yearning and effort at calm was becoming intolerable:

You cannot conceive how I ache to be with you: how I would die for one hour—for what is in the world? I say you cannot conceive; it is impossible you should look with such eyes upon me as I have upon you: it cannot be. You absorb me in spite of myself—you alone ... I hate the world: it batters too much the wings of my self-will, and would I could take a sweet poison from your lips to send me out of it.[88]

In trying to forget the world and Fanny's love, Keats falls back on his Self-will, using work as a means of escape. But the tension of being pulled two ways at once is clearly becoming too much of a strain. Two weeks later, on 5 August, he writes:

Thank God for my diligence! were it not for that I should be miserable. I encourage it, and strive not to think of you—but when I have succeeded in doing so all day and as far as midnight, you return as soon as this artificial excitement goes off more severely from the fever I am left in ... So you intend to hold me to my promise of seeing you in a short time. I shall keep it in as much sorrow as gladness: for I am not one of the Paladins of old who lived on water grass and smiles for years together—What though would I not give to night for the gratification of my eyes alone? ... This day week ... in [Brown's] absence I will flit to you and back. I will stay very little while; for as I am in a train of writing now I fear to disturb it—let it have its course bad or good—in it I shall try my own strength and the public pulse.[89]

Seeing Fanny would certainly have put at risk his 'artificial excitement', and he was afraid of disturbing the 'train of writing' he was in. The next letter to Fanny comes ten days later. As they had probably agreed to write weekly, this means that Keats had missed one letter. He writes:

I see you through a Mist: as I dare say you do me by this time. Believe in the first Letters I wrote you: I assure you I felt as I wrote—I could not write so now ... Remember I have had no idle leisure to brood over you—'it is well perhaps I have not—I could not have endured the throng of Jealousies that used to haunt me before I plunged so deeply into imaginary interests. I would feign, as my sails are set, sail on without interruption for a Brace of Months longer—I am in complete cue—in the fever; and shall in these four Months do an immense deal ... My heart seems now made of iron... I cannot help it—I am impell'd, driven to it. I am not happy enough for silken Phrases, and silver sentences.[90]

After breaking off for a page to describe Winchester, to which he had moved from Shanklin, he returned again to the theme that was preying on his mind:

> Forgive me this flint-worded Letter—and believe and see that I cannot think of you without some sort of energy—though mal a propos—Even as I leave off—it seems to me that a few more moments' thought of you would uncrystallize and dissolve me—I must not give way to it—but turn to my writing again—If I fail I shall die hard—O my love, your lips are growing sweet again to my fancy—I must forget them.[91]

In this letter Keats' attempt to wrest himself from the influence of his love had reached its extreme point, as had his almost feverish concentration on producing something for the presses. The tension he was feeling has mirrored itself in the very texture of the letters: they are 'flint-worded'. the phrases are, as he says, 'like so many strokes of a Hammer'.[92] After this letter of 16 August there is a gap of one month, and it seems more than probable that the reason is that Keats didn't write any. His next he wrote in London. He had been drawn there by a letter from America telling him that George was ruined. Keats wrote to Fanny, but he did not go to see her:

> Am I mad or not? I came by the Friday night coach—and have not yet been to Hampstead. Upon my soul it is not my fault, I cannot resolve to mix any pleasure with my days: they go one like another undistinguishable. If I were to see you today it would destroy the half comfortable sullenness I enjoy at present ... Knowing well that my life must be passed in fatigue and trouble, I have been endeavouring to wean myself from you.[93]

That last sentence is the key to the month of silence. Keats had, indeed, been endeavouring to wean himself from Fanny. This endeavour and its parallel, his pursuit with all his energy of the presses, forced on him by ever-increasing financial troubles, were destroying his creativity. To win Fanny, he had first to lose her. To 'compose' poetry, he had first to deny the very ground from which he knew poetry to spring. The torment of these paradoxes is clearly present in the letters of this time. And it was driving Keats away from Shakespeare and into the hands of Milton. He was doing exactly what Hazlitt says of Milton: 'He lived apart, in the solitude of his own thoughts, carefully excluding from his mind whatever might distract its purposes or alloy its purity, or damp its zeal'.[94]

Keats' ego was manifesting itself and was doing so in a great outpouring of productive energy—in a movement away from the natural creativity of Shakespeare in which the Self is annihilated and energy subsumed in Indolence. This movement away from Shakespeare can be seen in the letters written at this critical moment when the tensions were reaching crisis point. The first of these was to Bailey on 14 August, the second to Taylor on 23 August and the last to Reynolds on the following day. In these letters he did what he had not done in the ones to Fanny—he wrote directly about his creative life: 'I am convinced more and more every day that ... a fine writer is the most genuine Being in the World—Shakespeare and the paradise Lost every day become greater wonders to me—I look upon fine Phrases like a Lover'.[95] This is the first letter, to Bailey.

In the letter to Reynolds he uses virtually the same sentence, but there is a radical alteration and an even more radical omission: 'I am convinced more and more day by day that fine writing is next to fine doing the top thing in the world; the Paradise Lost becomes a greater wonder'.[96] The difference is small but dramatic. Shakespeare is no longer invoked along with Milton. Milton alone remains. Also, fine writing has taken second place to fine doing as the 'top thing in the world'. This is the end result of the process evidenced in all the letters of this period. It is the end result of Keats' refutation of his own better nature and of his belief in the creativity of Imagination that can be achieved in the moodlessness of diligent Indolence and Self-annihilation. He wrote to Taylor in the second of these letters: 'You will observe at the end of this if you put down the Letter "How a solitary life engenders Pride and egotism!" True: I know it does but this Pride and egotism will enable me to write finer things than any thing else could—so I will indulge it'.[97] In the last letter, he continued in the same vein: 'The more I know what my diligence may in time probably effect: the more does my heart distend with Pride and Obstinacy'.[98] Self-annihilation has here given way to a diligence directed towards an end—an effect—and the result is two of the sins of egotism: Pride and Obstinacy. The second half of this sentence contains an arresting quotation from 'Paradise Lost', a quotation of which Keats must have known the conclusion:

> And now his heart
> Distends with Pride, and hardning in his strength
> Glories[99]

This is exactly the tenor of these letters of Keats: the desperation of Satan revelling in the power of his forces; a desperate determination to believe that the course which circumstances had forced on him was the right one. This 'hardning' permits him to keep on course, even though he has dropped all of his poetic doctrines one by one. Self-annihilation has given way to the Pride and Obstinacy of ego; Indolence has given way to diligence; the immediacy of the silence in which alone language can speak has given way to the mediation of language as communication—a writing for the presses. And after this incomplete but telling quotation from Milton, Keats wrote: 'I feel it in my power to become a popular writer'.[100] In the earlier letter to Taylor he said: 'I feel every confidence that if I choose I may be a popular writer'.[101]

Negative capability, the 'quality which Shakespeare possessed so enormously'[102] and which depends crucially upon the annihilation of ego, has gone: 'My own being which I know to be becomes of more consequence to me than the crowds of Shadows in the Shape of Man and Women that inhabit a kingdom'.[103] Keats is now no longer 'unpoetical'; he is like 'Men and Women who . . . are poetical and have about them an unchangeable attribute'.[104] Thus far had he come from his own ideas on the 'poetical Character', which 'is not itself—it has no self—it is every thing and nothing—It has no character'.[105] Ambition, love and poetry were not now 'three ghosts',[106] 'shadows'[107] which come as 'masque-like figures on a dreamy urn',[108] but 'of more consequence . . . than the crowds of shadows'. Keats wanted to 'be dieted with praise'.[109]

By the middle of September Keats' suffering was reaching its peak. At just this point he heard that Kean, without whom 'Otho the Great' stood little chance of success, had gone off to America. At one blow his most realistic opportunity of making money had vanished. But this was not the end of his troubles. It was at this moment that he received the letter from America which was 'not of the brightest intelligence'[110] the letter saying that George was ruined. As a result of this, Keats took the coach to London on 10 September to see Abbey in the hope of raising some ready money to send to America. It was on this visit that he wrote to Fanny without going to Hampstead to see her: 'I am a Coward, I cannot bear the pain of being happy'.[111] Five days later he returned to Winchester. Brown, fortunately for us, was away in Ireland. Keats was left alone to mull over things. In these few days the profound tension that he had worked himself into snapped and the old serene, and Shakespearian, Keats re-emerged. At this point the ode 'To Autumn' was written and the revision of 'Hyperion' was abandoned. On 21 September he gave the reason to Reynolds: 'I have given up Hyperion—there were too many Miltonic inversions in it—Miltonic verse can not be written but in an artful or rather artist's humour'.[112]

Keats' effort to produce something for the presses was foreign to his natural poetic idiom and produced, through a conscious effort of will, poetry which was 'a corruption of our Language'.[113] Exceptional as it is, it has about it something forced, calculated, 'cut by feet'.[114] Keats now throws this aside in order to devote himself 'to another sensation'.[115] On the same day, 21 September, he wrote in his journal letter to America:

> I shall never become attach'd to a foreign idiom so as to put it into my writings. The Paradise lost though so fine in itself is a corruption of our Language—It should be kept as it is unique—a curiosity—a beautiful and grand Curiosity. The most remarkable Production of the world—A northern dialect accommodating itself to greek and latin inversions and intonations. The purest english I think—or what ought to be the purest—is Chatterton's—The Language had existed long enough to be entirely uncorrupted of Chaucer's gallicisms and still the old words are used—Chatterton's language is entirely northern—I prefer the native music of it to Milton's cut by feet I have but lately stood on my guard against Milton. Life to him would be death to me. Miltonic verse cannot be written but in the vein of art—I wish to devote myself to another sensation.[116]

And again, on the same day, to Reynolds:

> No I will not copy a parcel of verses. I always somehow associate Chatterton with Autumn. He is the purest writer in the English Language. He has no French idiom, or particles like Chaucer—'tis genuine English idiom in English words. I have given up

Hyperion—there were too many Miltonic inversions in it—Miltonic verse cannot be written but in an artful or rather artist's humour. I wish to give myself up to other sensations. English ought to be kept up. It may be interesting to you to pick out some lines from Hyperion and to put a mark × to the false beauty proceeding from art, and one‖ to the true voice of feeling.[117]

'English ought to be kept up', conscious writing 'for the presses' is a corruption of language, and language must be natural. It must come 'as naturally as the Leaves to a tree [or] it had better not come at all'. Language must not accommodate itself to foreign intonations, it must not be written 'in an artful or rather artist's humour'.

In these letters Chatterton stands in for Shakespeare, a comparison which Keats could make to his own poetry without discomfort. For Keats, Chatterton was the example, after Shakespeare, of the natural English poet, as the original dedication to 'Endymion' shows:

INSCRIBED,
WITH EVERY FEELING OF PRIDE AND REGRET,
AND WITH "A BOWED MIND,"
TO THE MEMORY OF
THE MOST ENGLISH OF POETS EXCEPT SHAKSPEARE,
THOMAS CHATTERTON.

The close relationship between Chatterton and Shakespeare in Keats' mind is seen also in the 'Epistle to George Felton Mathew':

Where we may soft humanity put on,
And sit, and rhyme and think on Chatterton;
And that warm-hearted Shakespeare sent to meet him
Four laurell'd spirits, heaven-ward to entreat him.[119]

In giving up 'Hyperion', Keats was giving up Milton for Shakespeare/Chatterton and the purity of natural language. He had succeeded in 'convincing [his] nerves'[120] that 'a fine writer is the most genuine Being in the World',[121] and that the fine writer is compromised in subsuming fine writing to fine doing.

In October, on Keats' return to London, he was called on by Severn who read 'Hyperion' and begged Keats to complete it, arguing that it was great enough to have been written by Milton. Keats replied that this was exactly the point: he did not want to put his name to a poem that might have been written by John Milton when he could put his name to one written by John Keats.[122]

Within a few days he was back in Hampstead.

6

The Fine Spell of Words

In a letter to Reynolds of 2 May 1818, Keats had compared human life to a 'large Mansion of Many Apartments':

> The first we step into we call the infant or thoughtless Chamber, in which we remain as long as we do not think—We remain there a long while, and notwithstanding the doors of the second Chamber remain wide open, showing a bright appearance, we care not to hasten to it; but are at length, imperceptibly impelled by the awakening of this thinking principle—within us—we no sooner get into the second Chamber, which I shall call the Chamber of Maiden-Thought, than we become intoxicated with the light and the atmosphere, we see nothing but pleasant wonders, and think of delaying there for ever in delight: However among the effects this breathing is father of is that tremendous one of sharpening one's vision into the heart and nature of Man—of convincing ones nerves that the World is full of Misery and Heartbreak, Pain, Sickness and oppression—whereby this Chamber of Maiden Thought becomes gradually darken'd and at the same time on all sides of it many doors are set open—but all dark—all leading to dark passages—we see not the ballance of good and evil. We are in a mist. *We* are now in that state—We feel the 'burden of the Mystery'.[1]

Looking into the dark passages leading from the Chamber of Maiden Thought, the poet is as if 'in a mist' and cannot see 'the ballance of good and evil'. For hints of this balance Keats turns to Wordsworth, for 'his Genius is explorative of those dark Passages'.[2] Keats realised, even at this early point, that Milton had failed to reach even this stage: 'Here I must think Wordsworth is deeper than Milton ... From the Paradise Lost and the other Works of Milton, I hope it is not too presuming, even between ourselves to say, his Philosophy, human and divine, may be tolerably understood by one not much advanced in years'.[3]

For Keats, Milton is the poet of the 'Chamber of Maiden Thought', a chamber from which Keats had to pass, because his vision was sharpened into 'the heart and nature of Man' by the world of 'Misery and Heartbreak, Pain, Sickness and oppression'. In this world lies the path which he promises to travel.

It is in the revision of 'Hyperion' that we can see Keats following this path. His attempt at Miltonic composition had been for him the greatest peril. He had been trying to 'find a haven in the world',[4] to be a poet by a conscious effort of will, and it was exactly in doing so that he was saved. In Miltonic composition he had discovered his own retreat from the dream that when 'he awoke he found it truth'.[5] In the letter to Reynolds he says: 'It may be interesting to you to pick out some lines from Hyperion and put a mark ✕ to the false beauty proceeding from art, and one ‖ to the true voice of feeling'.[6] Composition 'in an artful or rather artist's humour'[7] gathers its completion to itself before it has begun: the poem is revealed prior to the language in which it is spoken, and thus the challenge is put to language to supply the poem. As Hazlitt says of Shakespeare: 'His plays ... are properly expressions ... not descriptions'.[8] Dreaming and composition are two poles of the same dimension: the letting of language speak and the using of language to speak. Both of these are ways of revealing—but radically different ones. Yet, for the poet, it may be that within the peril of straining towards the latter lies the key to saving the former. Lying in wait within the process of the willing of composition, the process in which the freedom of the poet is surrendered along with language to the composition of the poem, is the threat to his freedom which, felt as a threat, as a restriction, grants him his freedom again. Even a running from the peril is an admission of the peril. Shakespeare circles in Milton's orbit.

This discovery of his own freedom, of Shakespeare, was lying in wait for Keats during his plunge into the Miltonic peril and was itself a part of that plunge. Keats' continual return to Milton was an escape from Shakespeare, which is present in 1817, in 'Endymion', in the Spring Odes and now, once again, in the revision of 'Hyperion'.

The ostensible story of this poem is the revolt of the Titans, but one of the strangest things to be noted is that the poem breaks off once this tale is under way. Once the gods can tell their tale, the poet falls silent. The poem is an uncovering of this silence—of the path towards the mystery—of the poet's journey. In outline it is as follows:

The poet enters a garden of Eden, where he discovers the remnants of a meal which has been eaten, as it seems to him, by an angel. He feels the craving of an appetite stronger than he has ever felt on earth and eats deliciously, and then immediately thirsts. He drinks from a vessel of transparent juice and falls into a swoon. When he wakes, he finds himself in a stone temple unlike any he had ever seen. Far away, to the west, he sees an image on an altar towards which he goes slowly, its holiness filling him with bliss. Yet, as he arrives at the shrine, an awful pronouncement warns him that he will die if he cannot reach the steps of the altar before the leaves of incense are burnt. He struggles forward, passing as he does so through all the sensations of dying, and only at the moment before death does his foot touch the altar steps and life flow into him again.

He asks the veiled priestess why his life has been returned to him, and she answers that it is because he has the power to feel:

> What 'tis to die and live again before
> Thy fated hour[9]

Still not understanding, he asks for more enlightenment, and the priestess answers that the only people who can be saved as he has been saved are:

> those to whom the miseries of the world
> Are misery, and will not let them rest[10]

He then asks why he alone is there, and she replies that only weak dreamers may enter there. Simple lovers of their fellow men, simple doers of good, have no thought of entering, but dreamers are rewarded for the extremity of their suffering by finding safety at the feet of the statue. The poet then asks whose the temple is and is answered that it is Saturn's temple, that he is standing at Saturn's feet and that the priestess is:

> Moneta, left supreme
> Sole priestess of his desolation.[11]

Moneta then offers to show her face, until now hidden behind veils, and he describes the vision that he sees. Finally, he asks to behold:

> What in thy brain so ferments to and fro[12]

What he sees there is the tale of the revolt of the Titans, the tale begun in the original 'Hyperion' of a year before. At this point the poem fades slowly to an end. Keats went on to write the ode 'To Autumn'.

This bare outline of the poem tells us little other than that it is about the poet's path towards the vision of a mystery. At the opening of the poem the gods have been vanquished—the Titans have been destroyed. The gods are helpless and can no longer save the poet; they can no longer offer their power to aid his dull mortality:

> For heaven is parted from thee, and the earth
> Knows thee not, so afflicted, for a God.[13]

This power is now a curse to the gods—a desolation. Moneta, the Mnemosyne of the first 'Hyperion', is left as sole priestess of the temple in which the fallen Saturn lies. She is:

> Sole priestess of his desolation[14]

A desolation in which the god can no longer gather the poet to himself and grant him the gift of poetic utterence. The poet is silent:

> I had no words to answer; for my tongue,
> Useless, could find about its roofed home
> No syllable of fit majesty.[15]

Without speech the poet is lost, and the vanquished gods, from their desolation, can grant nothing more than that desolation. And, if the gift is not granted to the poet, then how much more is lost to the rest of us? The poet knows this and asks:

> Are there not thousands in the world
> ....
> Who love their fellows even to the death;
> Who feel the giant agony of the world;
> And more, like slaves to poor humanity,
> Labour for mortal good?[16]

These mortals, slaving for the good of their fellows, cannot recognise the gift of poetic speech, even though they labour, knowing they labour to an end. Further, they cannot even recognise the desolation of the gods as a desolation; they cannot experience the desolation for what it is:

> They come not here, they have no thought to come[17]

They turn from it and sink themselves into the world, seeking other things:

> They seek no wonder but the human face;
> No music but the happy-noted voice[18]

Mortals, in their inability to recognise the desolation as desolation—as what it is—also fail to recognise the nature of their own mortality. However, such mortals can also be those:

> Who feel the giant agony of the world;
> And more, like slaves to poor humanity,
> Labour for mortal good

Mortals can assert themselves and may do so 'for mortal good', but by this assertion they do not achieve security. In the very taking of decisions, in the very certainty of their decisiveness, they leave the result in the balance.

Mortals dwell in the world. The world for them is a dwelling in the modern sense of the word: a permanent place of safety and security. Their decisiveness lies in this direction. Yet the original significance of the word lies hidden at the core of this facile security. Dwelling is a leading astray, a being in error, a holding in place temporarily, a hindrance. Here, at the heart of its safety, lies an insecurity, an error. Mortal decision-making is a temporary holding in place, an insecurity which lies, unreckoned, at the heart of its desperate searching for security. The very searching implies it.

Keats calls 'The Fall of Hyperion' a dream. 'Dream' is a key word for Keats, and especially so in this poem. 'Dream', in the sense of 'delusion' or 'deceptive appearance', not necessarily in sleep, has its source in the Early Middle English 'dream', 'drem' and probably also relates back to the Old English 'dréam'. Dream is an appearance, a showing of something hidden. Attempts have been made to relate it back to the Greek *thrumos*, meaning 'joyful music', 'exhilaration', 'clamour', 'a jubilare'.

The searcher, the mortal, is a dreamer and his search for security is a search for the real, for reality, for what exists. It is a search undertaken by all mortals, by all who dwell on earth. And yet, now the mortal sets himself up against his own mortality and adopts the secure reality of his dreams. This modern searcher, who dredges up a security from out of his dreams, Keats calls a fanatic:

> Fanatics have their dreams, wherewith they weave
> A paradise for a sect.[19]

These are the opening lines of the poem. 'Dreams' here means 'delusions', but delusions that are so much of a delusion that they are no longer even recognised as such. Delusion is the mortal shadow of the desolation of the holy. Fanatics make a paradise for a sect. They cut off the secure delusion from the desolation of the holy—a not too difficult movement, as the holy is no longer even recognised as desolate—and formulate it into a dogma for a sect; that is to say, not for all mortals. In this sectarian security the mortal is cut off from his own mortality as well as from the holy. This formulation, or dogma, can only be written in 'an artful or rather artist's humour'. It is from this sectarian and deluded security that Milton suffers. His reality is 'a paradise for a sect', a paradise of 'hammer strokes' 'cut by feet', a paradise 'woven', not out of language even, but out of the materials of the dreams themselves. It is a process which takes up the threads of a dream and manipulates them into a pattern, clearly visible.

The poem continues:

> the savage too
> From forth the loftiest fashion of his sleep
> Guesses at Heaven[20]

The savage is neither fanatic nor poet, and yet he 'guesses at heaven'. Their dwelling is not the secure dream of delusion but a mortal dwelling that is a finite holding in place which can thus dream of the immortal. Death is no longer cut off from them as it is from the fanatic. It is death that places the mortal in his dwelling place and thus enables him to 'guess at Heaven'. They are not in a deluded security and yet neither are they in the safety of insecurity. Their security is their dwelling place, and they can therefore guess at heaven, but only guess because their dream is not yet a vision. Unable to renounce the words, they are left only with the words' shadows. This is why:

> these have not
> Trac'd upon vellum wild Indian leaf
> The shadows of melodious utterance[21]

Dream as utterance, as jubilare, is not for them. The word withdraws itself, and they are left with its shadows only: they die 'bare of laurels'.[22] Yet, they do not live only for a sect but are those:

> Who love their fellows even to the death;
> Who feel the giant agony of the world;
> And more, like slaves to poor humanity,
> Labour for human good.[23]

They labour, and they do so for the good of their fellow mortals, but even so they are not masters but slaves. They dwell in their insecurity. Of these the poet can only say, simply, that 'they live, dream and die'.[24] and he adds immediately:

> For Poesy alone can tell her dreams.[25]

Only for the poet can the dream become an utterance, only through him can imagination be saved. It is 'the fine spell of words'[26] that draws the dream from 'dumb enchantment'[27] into the realm of safety:

> For Poesy alone can tell her dreams

Poesy alone, and not the poet, can let the dream be what it is, can show what is hidden. Poesy:

> With the fine spell of words alone can save
> Imagination from the sable charm
> And dumb enchantment.[28]

The poet's imagination is saved, and the saviour is none other than the 'fine spell of words'. The saviour is the spell of words—the spell that gathers together the words in such a way that they become fine. Spell here is not merely a spelling, the correct arrangement of the letters; it is not merely the correct form of the words. Within this signification is contained another. In the correct breaking down of the word into its individual letters is hidden the splitting or cleaving apart of the words. We have this meaning in the expression 'working for a spell' or 'taking a spell at work'. The spell or shift breaks the whole down into its parts and also gathers those parts into a relationship. The saviour is the spell of words. The word gathers itself together in a spell. A further signification of this word is the gathering together of words into an incantation which, if we place ourselves within it, grants us occult or mysterious power. The saviour is the spell of words which is the power granted to the poet. Not a power over the words but the power to be saved by the spell of words.

Unlike the fanatic whose dwelling is a deluded security, whose words are dogma 'for a sect', who feels secure even against death and whose own mortality is as unknown to him as is the desolation of the gods; unlike the savage who dwells in the world of mortality, of finitude, and who can thus merely 'guess at heaven'—the poet is in the safety of insecurity.

The poet dwells within the spell of words, and thus the opportunity opens itself for him to dwell within the safety of insecurity; that is, within the safety of his own mortality. This power to be saved—the power of the spell—is the power that saves from death. Death is that part of life which belongs to the spell as its other side. Without it the spell is nothing more than a shift which we can secure deludedly as fanatic or pass over insecurely as savage. The poet has first of all to refute the 'world's gaudy ensigns'[29]—verse, fame and beauty (the 'Love, Ambition and Poetry' of the 'Ode on Indolence'[30])—and it is death that does so for him:

> Verse, Fame, and Beauty are intense indeed,
> But Death intenser—Death is Life's high meed.[31]

Keats wrote these lines back in March 1819. As seen from life, in Miltonic Self-certainty, insecurity is nothing more than the break in the spell and appears as negative; death in this way also becomes negative. The fanatic arms himself against it with dogma and makes himself secure. The savage in his insecurity can only 'guess at heaven'. The poet, however, staying within the spell, within the Contraries, destroys the Negations and redeems the Contraries, which are the play of the spell.[32] Death is transformed from Negation to Contrary, and imagination is saved from silence—from remaining dumb—by the poet's refusal to secure it.

> Thou hast felt
> What 'tis to die and live again before
> Thy fated hour. That thou hadst power to do so
> Is thy own safety.[33]

Death is the ultimate mystery of the suffering of the world, the suffering which, deeply thought on, gradually darkens the Chamber of Maiden Thought. The light and atmosphere of this chamber has the effect of 'sharpening one's vision into the heart and nature of Man—of convincing one's nerves that the World is full of Misery and Heartbreak, Pain, Sickness and oppression'.[34] The passages leading from this chamber become gradually darkened, because 'we see not the ballance of good and evil',[35] which is the mere balance of the Negations and not the spell of the Contraries and cannot, therefore, be redeemed. Our inability to see this balance leaves us in a mist, feeling the 'burden of the Mystery'.[36] This mystery is the mystery of suffering, whose spell we cannot dwell in. The ultimate suffering is death, which is the mere Negation of life and which cannot yet be seen as that part of life which belongs to the spell as its other side. Beyond this the fanatic or the savage cannot reach. Unlike them, the poet does not refute the Negation and take it as mere Negation, but redeems it as Contrary and dwells within it in the midst of its spell. He:

> venoms all his days,
> Bearing more woe than all his sins deserve[37]

He is a 'fever of [him]self'[38] and is told:

> None can usurp this height ...
> But those for whom the miseries of the world
> Are misery and will not let them rest.[39]

The poet, by Self-annihilation, redeems the Contraries and stands within the agony of the spell:

> As to the poetical Character itself ... it is not itself—it has no self—it is every thing and nothing—It has no Character ... A Poet is the most unpoetical of any thing in existence; because he has no Identity ... the

Sun, the Moon, the Sea and Men and Women who are creatures of impulse are poetical and have about them an unchangeable attribute—the poet has none; no identity—he is certainly the most unpoetical of all God's Creatures.[40]

The poet, annihilating ego, comes within the spell. The fanatic creates dogma to hide himself from his mortality. The savage may indeed:

> love their fellows even to the death;
> Who feel the giant agony of the world;
> And more, like slaves to poor humanity,
> Labour for human good

but:

> They come not here, they have no thought to come.[41]

The poet comes because he is a 'dreamer weak'.[42] He comes in 'sickness'[43] and 'unworthiness'[44] because he is 'less than they'.[45] He has no identity. 'He was the least of an egotist that it was possible to be'.[46] He has no 'unchangeable attribute'. The fanatic is secure in his Self-hood, the savage insecure in his, but the poet annihilates his Self and, in doing so, becomes 'less than they'. Dwelling within the spell, the poet is a 'fever of [him]self' and 'venoms all his days'. This is what the poet is told:

> Think of the Earth;
> What bliss even in hope is there for thee?
> What haven? every creature hath its home;
> Every sole man hath days of joy and pain,
> Whether his labours be sublime or low—
> The pain alone; the joy alone; distinct.[47]

The poet has no haven on earth as has every other one of God's creatures. He does not know distinct moments of joy and pain. He cannot have his home on earth, as he cannot face away from pain and suffering, separating life and death, joy and pain, into distinct regions. This 'haven', the haven that Keats was searching for in his 'artful or rather artist's humour', where the differences have been refined into

distinct principles, is denied him. Where Milton, 'took only a few
simple principles and raised them to the utmost conceivable grandeur,
and refined them from every base alloy'.[48] he cannot, he is unable to:

> unperplex bliss from its neighbour pain;
> Define their pettish limits, and estrange
> Their points of contact, and swift counterchange;
> Intrigue with the specious chaos, and dispart
> Its most ambiguous atoms with sure art[49]

In this calculated refining the spell is broken into its Negations, where
the search for the balance of good and evil can take place. But this
search is fruitless for the poet, however much he might desire it:

> never will the prize,
> High reason, and the lore of good and ill
> Be my award. Things cannot to the will
> Be settled but they tease us out of thought.[50]

Thus unprotected, the poet struggles within the spell, dwells there in
his insecurity and, redeeming the Contraries, is saved.

Yet the saviour is none other than the struggle within this insecurity;
it is the 'fine spell of words'. The spell is the magical reward of itself
and in no way a means to an end. It is itself its own end and, recurring
continually in this grounding signification, it is fine. Dwelling within
the fine spell, the holy and the sacrilegious circle within the mutual
attraction of each other's gravity. This is the region in which the poet
can say 'I am here alone'.[51] He is in the region where other men, fanatic
or savage, 'have no thought to come'.

A year earlier Keats has written the extraordinary letter to his
brother and sister-in-law in America in which it is possible to read
hints of the path which he still had to travel:

Even here though I myself am pursueing the same instinctive course as
the veriest human animal you can think of . . . without knowing the
bearing of any one assertion of any one opinion. Yet may I not in this
be free from sin? May there not be superior beings amused with any
graceful, though instinctive attitude my mind may fall into, as I am
entertained with the alertness of the Stoat or the anxiety of a Deer?
Though a quarrel in the streets is a thing to be hated, the energies

displayed in it are fine; the commonest Man shows a grace in his
quarrel—By a superior being our reasonings may take the same
tone—though erroneous they may be fine—This is the very thing in
which consists poetry; and if so it is not so fine a thing as
philosophy—For the same reason that an eagle is not so fine a thing as
a truth—Give me this credit—Do you not think I strive—to know
myself? Give me this credit—and you will not think that on my
account I repeat Milton's lines:

> 'How charming is divine Philosophy
> Not harsh and crabbed as dull fools suppose
> But musical as is Apollo's lute'[52]

In this difficult passage the key word 'fine' appears in almost every
sentence, and Keats includes the vital comment: 'This is the very thing
in which consists poetry'. Keats uses the word 'fine' at key moments to
express something of the feeling of Blake's 'Energy', an Energy which,
although at first seen as preferable to Reason—as one side of the
warring of Self against not-Self—is later recognised as the struggle
taking place within the Self. The Energy of Milton's description of
Hell, in comparison to his description of Heaven, is recognised by
Keats exactly as it was by Blake, a poet whom Keats almost certainly
never read. In Book III of 'Paradise Lost' are these lines:

> Thus while God spoke, ambrosial fragrance fill'd
> All heaven, and in the blessed Spirits elect
> Sense of new joy ineffable diffus'd[53]

In the margin of his copy, Keats wrote: 'Hell is finer than this'.[54]

This whole section of the letter is pregnant with echoes of Blake.
'Energy is Eternal Delight'.[55] 'Though a quarrel in the streets is a thing
to be hated, the energies displayed in it are fine'.[56] The energies which
are fine give grace to even the commonest man. A superior being
would recognise that it is not a question of right or wrong but of
Energy. The lare of good and ill, the balance of good and evil, can
never be the poet's award. And yet this reasoning, this balance, though
erroneous, may be fine. 'This is the very thing in which consists poetry'
—'a fine writer is the most genuine Being in the world'.[57] Adam's
dream was of the fineness of this Energy, and 'he awoke and found it
truth'.[58] The poet's indolent dream—Adam's dream—had bridged the

gap between the mortal and the immortal, and when he awoke he found the words, the poem, to be truth. Somehow the gap between the mortal and the immortal had been bridged by the dream, and yet Keats recognised that the gap itself remained and that the very bridging of it admitted of its existence, drew it into existence. This poetry, which is fine, 'is not so fine a thing as philosophy',[59] which is the same thing but as its other side—the side in which an eagle becomes a truth. In this moment, the holy and the sacrilegious are held in the spell, but as Negations—the saviour is not to hand. In this letter Keats is straining over the gap towards the holy—'straining at particles of light in the midst of a great darkness'.[60] There is only an extrinsic recognition of the gods' desolation.

The final passage of the first 'Hyperion' was completed at just this moment. The letter and the poem are in parallel; the argument is the same. Mnemosyne leaves the fallen gods to give nurture to Apollo (to the Keats of the later revision), and the knowledge he thus gains bridges the gap between the sacrilegious and the holy. Here, in the first 'Hyperion', it is by the grant of knowledge from the holy, from Mnemosyne, that the poet, Apollo, is himself transformed into the holy. The holy, the sacred, grants its secret to the poet and yet, in granting, transformed it:

> 'Why should I tell thee what thou so well seest?
> 'Why should I strive to show what from thy lips
> 'Would come no mystery?[61]

From the lips of the god the sacred would be revealed and lose its secret; it would no longer be itself.[62] The poet remains visionless—'painful vile oblivion seals my eyes'[63]—and desolate:

> 'Like one who once had wings'[64]

The poet had already sensed the creation of the word through its renunciation, but this had always been in a dream. In the Self-annihilation of Indolence the imagination had revealed truth, whether it existed before or not:

> 'Goddess! I have beheld those eyes before,
> 'And their eternal calm, and all that face,
> 'Or I have dream'd'.—'Yes', said the supreme shape

> 'Thou hast dream'd of me; and awaking up
> 'Didst find a lyre all golden by thy side,
> 'Whose strings touch'd by thy fingers, all the vast
> 'Unwearied ear of the whole universe
> 'Listen'd in pain and pleasure at the birth
> 'Of such new tuneful wonder'.[65]

Apollo had dreamed of Mnemosyne, and he awoke to find it truth. He had been granted the mortal insecurity of safety and yet:

> there grew
> A power within me of enormous ken,
> To see as a God sees.[66]

This knowledge, which is in the grant of the gods, is granted to the poet, to Apollo, and he accepts it. He who 'once had wings' senses a renewal and demands the secret from behind the veil of the sacred:

> Point me out the way
> To any one particular beauteous star
> And I will flit into it with my lyre,
> And make its silvery splendour pant with bliss.[67]

Here, as in the 'Ode to a Nightingale', Keats realised that the demand of Apollo could not be met without destroying the very thing demanded. There is nothing here of the fine spell of words, but there is a finitus. As in the letter, the spell remains a mere break, a split between the sacrilegious and the holy. A saviour does indeed reveal itself, but it is the safety of a holy security. The poet cannot finally recognise the desolation of the gods in his time, at least here. The poem is indeed about the fall of Hyperion, but the poet does not enter the spell, and the safety of the holy grant remains the safety of security. Keats/Apollo annihilates Self and enters into a holy safety secure in a 'knowledge enormous',[68] which is the grant of the gods—a grant of immortality to the mortal. Mnemosyne remains silent, but her silence is articulate, and it is the grant of a knowledge that immortalises Apollo:

'Mute thou remainest—Mute! yet I can read
'A wondrous lesson in thy silent face
'Knowledge enormous makes a God of me[69]

Apollo 'die[s] into life'[70] because of the grant of this 'knowledge enormous'. The lesson he read in the face of Mnemosyne is what, once learnt, enables the gap to be bridged and the poet to be granted godhead:

'Names, deeds, gray legends, dire events, rebellions,
'Majesties, sovran voices, agonies,
'Creations and destroyings, all at once
'Pour into the wide hollows of my brain,
'And deify me[71]

Apollo is transformed from a mortal poet safe within his own mortal insecurity to the safe security of the immortal:

Soon wild commotions shook him, and made flush
All the immortal fairness of his limbs;
Most like the struggle at the gate of death;
Or liker still to one who should take leave
Of pale immortal death, and with a pang
As hot as death's is chill, with fierce convulse
Die into life: so young Apollo anguish'd.[72]

At the last, the spell had been broken. It was not Keats who had been granted the gift of immortality, for the poet was too honest to the nature of poetry to permit this. Apollo dies into immortal life but leaves the poet where he was. Nothing else was possible. Any continuation of the poem would have been a lie, and thus it finishes here. Keats was still a mortal poet. A different kind of poem would have to tell what Mnemosyne's silence granted to the poet; what he here sees as:

A wondrous lesson in thy silent face.[73]

In the first 'Hyperion' the spell of words was broken. Mnemosyne remained mute. Apollo, learning the wondrous lesson, bridged the gap opened up by a break in the spell and became immortal—an immortality only possible, however, because the poet had yet to recognise that the desolation and the power to save are not the gods' alone. Apollo was on the other side and could discourse with the gods. The poet, remaining where he was, broke off the poem; the authority to proceed was not his.

But, in the year that followed, a further movement took place. Leaving behind him the dreams of fanatic and savage, and even of Apollo, the poet entered the fine spell of words. The dream is now Keats' own. The wondrous lesson which is read in the silent face of Mnemosyne and which gave to Apollo the 'knowledge enormous', with which he rose to the ranks of the immortal, is now granted to the poet himself—and directly. But now there is a radical difference: the poet does not break the spell. The 'knowledge enormous' is not here the knowledge of the mystery by which the secret held within the gift of the sacred can be beheld. Here, the poet is no longer beholden to the gods for this. He dies into life, indeed, but the power to do so is his own, and the life is his own also:

> Thou hast felt
> What 'tis to die and live again before
> Thy fated hour. That thou hadst power to do so
> Is thy own safety[74]

He himself, Keats the poet, is within the spell. He has found no haven in the world. He is not the fanatic who lives within the mortal security of his safety, which is the security of dogma. Nor is he the dreaming savage who is insecure in his mortality and can thus only guess at heaven. He has travelled further than these, moving further along the poetic path—further even than the Apollo of the first 'Hyperion'. His dying into life is no longer a movement from one side to the other, a movement which sees the spell as gap, as distance to be bridged. The seductive pull of the holy that draws the poet over the gap, that gives him the gap as distance, is the greatest peril. It is a peril that leads at best to the poetry of vindication, of the zealot with a message, and to the corruption of language, to something unique, maybe to 'a beautiful and grand Curiosity',[75] but to a 'foreign idiom' nonetheless. Yet in this peril the saviour lies hidden, for vindication which wants to close the gap can never be in alliance with the Self-annihilation of Indolence. The poet renounces the 'knowledge enormous' and, in renunciation, is granted the spell. Keats is not now dreaming of immortality or speaking of immortality. The wondrous message he now reads in the face of Moneta—a new, latinised and altogether sterner Mnemosyne—is radically altered. Keats is a dreamer who 'venoms all his days'[76] and to whom Moneta can say:

> thou art
> A fever of thyself[77]

The poet is no Apollo who can be granted and accept the gift of godhead or the gift of language. The entire history of Keats' poetic output is the history of his slow but persistent realisation of this. The poet now sees that he is merely; that is, purely himself—what he is and no more. With the revision of 'Hyperion' comes the recognition of what it means for the poet Keats to be purely himself. He does indeed read a 'knowledge enormous' in the face of Moneta, but the knowledge does not grant him godhead. It grants him merely the renunciation of the holy; or rather, it is the renunciation of the holy that is itself the 'knowledge enormous'. It is only in the weakness of renunciation that the grant of the holy can be born and, what is the same thing, that the grant of language can be silenced. The poet is one of the 'dreamers weak'[78] and 'less'[79] than fanatic or savage, because he is what he truly is and nothing more, and lets the grant of the gods be what it is:

> Without stay or prop
> But my own weak mortality, I bore
> The load of this eternal quietude[80]

This itself is the power which is the poet's own safety:

> That thou hadst power to do so
> Is thy own safety[81]

and enables him to be where he is and exist within the 'fine spell of words'.

This is the vision which Moneta grants the poet or, rather, which the poet grants himself in the vision of Moneta. The god, in the desolation of the poet's epoch, lifts the veil which curtains her in mysteries and reveals her face, which is the vision of the desolation of the holy:

> But yet I had a terror of her robes,
> And chiefly of the veils, that from her brow
> Hung pale, and curtain'd her in mysteries
> That made my heart too small to hold its blood.
> This saw that Goddess, and with sacred hand
> Parted the veils. Then saw I a wan face,
> Not pin'd by human sorrows, but bright-blanch'd
> By an immortal sickness which kills not;
> It works a constant change, which happy death
> Can put no end to; deathwards progressing
> To no death was that visage; it had pass'd
> The lilly and the snow; and beyond these
> I must not think now, though I saw that face—
> But for her eyes I should have fled away.
> They held me back, with a benignant light,
> Soft-mitigated by divinest lids
> Half closed, and visionless entire they seem'd
> Of all external things—they saw me not,
> But in blank splendour beam'd like the mild moon,
> Who comforts those she sees not, who knows not
> what eyes are upward cast.[82]

The two sides of the spell are here the spell itself. Death, that part of life that belongs to the spell as its other side, is here wholly itself; that is, itself as holy. Moneta's face is not:

> pin'd by human sorrows, but bright blanch'd
> By an immortal sickness

a sickness:

> which happy death
> Can put no end to

while the poet prays:

> Intense, that Death would take me from the vale
> And all its burthens[83]

This it cannot do, for the very power to be safe within the insecurity is the poet's. It is he who:

> hast felt
> What 'tis to die and live again before
> Thy fated hour. That thou hadst power to do so
> Is thy own safety; thou hast dated on
> Thy doom

The poet has 'die[d] into life'[84] and is saved from death. The gap that Apollo bridged in becoming immortal in the first 'Hyperion', the gap over which the poet yearned for the heard melody of the nightingale, is now the fine spell in which the poet's path lies. The Negations have been destroyed to redeem the Contraries, which are 'deities or mortals'. In the agony of the spell the poet is drawn away from his vision, which at the very same instant draws him back:

> But for her eyes I should have fled away.
> They held me back with a benignant light

and yet this light is itself:

> Soft-mitigated by divinest lids.

The benign light is only partly visible. The 'divinest lids' are 'half closed' over it, and the eyes themselves are visionless:

> They saw me not
> But in blank splendour beam'd

In the spell of the Contraries the veil is lifted; the poet holds himself within the spell in his own weak mortality, which has nonetheless dated on its doom. Being merely what he is, a 'dreamer weak', 'less' than fanatic or savage, sustained by nothing less than his own weak mortality, he bears the load. This load is the eternal quietude, which is within the spell of the renunciation of the word, and yet he is, nonetheless, 'the most genuine being in the world'—'a fine writer'. This is the wondrous lesson beheld in the silent face of Moneta which the poet had been promised in the first 'Hyperion'. This is the 'silent form [that] dost tease us out of thought'.[86] In holding himself within the spell the poet is granted the gift which he has first renounced, and in this renunciation the gods come to be—come into a recognition of their own desolation—and the poem falls to a close. The poet bears:

> The load of this eternal quietude[87]

until, miraculously:

> old Saturn rais'd his faded eyes,
> And look'd around and saw his kingdom gone[88]

The poet, in the agony of the spell, is granted a vision of the first inkling of the making whole, of the redemption of the holy—which is the spell as its other side. This event is as a dream ('The Fall of Hyperion, a Dream')[89] which 'when he awoke he found it truth'. The poet, who is 'a fever of [him]self' and 'venoms all his days', lives and dies into life within the orbit of the sacrilegious. This knowledge draws the poet into the spell's insecurity and gives him the power to save the holy along with himself, to save the holy which is nothing without himself—to draw the holy also into the spell. At risk in the spell, they can dream truth which is beauty and 'all ye know on earth'.[90] The poet who will not let the misery of the world rest, who will not let death rest, holds himself within the spell in which the holy can also hold itself and recognise itself for what it is, which in our epoch is a desolation.

7

Interface

In reading Keats, one is drawn along the critical path in two related ways, because Keats is both poet and critic.

As critic, he is thinker and carries on a dialogue with poetry. As thinker, he avoids the destructive assault of an analysis of poetry, because he knows the value of poetry and dreads its destruction. He recognises what the analyst fails to understand, that poetry creates itself and cannot be recreated over again in terms alien to its own. The great poet is the great critic and reading Keats in his Miltonic or critical incarnation means being involved in a dialogue between thinker and thinker. This dialogue draws the thinker into critique.

Our reading of Keats' poetry mirrors this Miltonic dialogue, which draws us into the poetry. It is a dialogue of thinker and poet in which we come to recognise what Keats recognised, that critique has always already collapsed in the face of the poem's refusal to succumb.

For thinkers, these two dialogues—with the thinker and with the poet—are the only ones possible. Each involves as much listening as speaking. But in Keats the distinction is sometimes blurred, and this blurring puts us on our guard. Thinking about thinking we are sometimes disarmed and drawn into the poem. Reading the poem we sometimes find ourselves back with critique. The two are close, and this makes critique particularly unnerving. This distinction highlights the critical problem and forces the critic to ask himself what he is doing. The Postface which follows is an attempt to face up to this demand.

8

Postface: The Critic As Servant

Criticism, like translation, is always from one language into another and involves knowing the text in a new way. When criticism aims to be objective, it holds the text off at a distance and clarifies it in a language other than its own. This new language mediates between text and critic, destroying the immediate experience of the language of the poem and transforming it into something else. It reverses the experience in which the language of the poem is its text and nothing else, in which the text of the poem is its own pretext and needs no other.

The words of the poem are understood by us in spite of any analysis of them. Truth 'is not compelling through reason but through life. The truth of a poem is compelling because we experience it and not because we can trace out a reason for its being so'.[1] Although reflection can enhance the artistic experience, it is nonetheless always the result of such an experience. In trying to criticise the poem, we withdraw from the quite distinct knowledge we already have that what we are criticising is poetic. The poem is dissipated in the face of an assault made upon it by the critical method. The text is put to use and is used up. It becomes, from the very first, that which the critical process ends up making it. It becomes a phantom.[2]

This critical technique is appropriate in an age in which technology is supreme. Just as agricultural cultivation is now an assault upon the land, an assault which challenges it to produce food for consumption, so the critic challenges the poetic text to produce revelations, insights, truths. What can be produced from the land or the poem is the justification of their existence. Like agriculture, criticism is becoming an industry. And yet agriculture implies something else. For the peasant, it is a taking care of the field, country or land which concerns him. Far from treating the land as merely one element in a production process, he gives his seeds into the care of the earth, which retains to itself the forces of increase.[3] Is it possible that the same is true of the poem which, perhaps, will give back to the critic only insofar as he entrusts himself to its care. Gathering together through an assault is indicative of a dislocation in the natural order of things. Fundamental to this dislocation is a view of man as active subject, who puts knowing in the service of doing—the cognitive in the service of the conative—and judges knowledge in terms of what can be done with it. The poem is no longer attended *on* but attended *to*, and the quest for the poem becomes a question demanding a response.

THE CRITIC

The critic is in the service of the reader and serves the text. The text reserves itself for his observation.

The kind of service which the critic does to the text by his observation is the sort of revealing which lies at the core of modern criticism—a revealing by a process of questioning. Observation is an ob-serving. The 'ob' here means 'against' or 'in the way of'. The kind of serving which ob-serves, keeps the poem in view but as something in the way, something which has to be overcome and verified. The analytic critical process is an observing questioning of the text, which conserves itself as method and passes on leaving the poem behind. Poetic revealing, on the other hand, brings into preservation—that is, into the protection of the reader—that which, by its very nature holds itself in reserve. The critic can thus serve the text in one of two ways: one conserves, the other preserves. 'Con-serving' means 'to save', 'to keep by (*con*) adding things', 'to keep by changing the nature of what is to be saved'. To make marmalade the oranges are thickened and solidified with sugar. Pre-serving, on the other hand, means 'to protect from change', 'to keep from harm', 'to maintain', 'to keep free from trespass', 'to keep pristine', that is, 'to keep as it was (*pre*) at first'.

Modern criticism's way of con-serving ob-serves the text in a questioning assault and can thus reproduce the text only in terms of those categories in which the questioning is framed; the critic keeps by adding alien elements. Military cartographers sometimes use an overlay—a sketch on transparent plastic of some specific feature such as the deployment of forces—which is placed over the ordinary map and keyed to it. The only way that the real map can be read is through the overlay, and the region is then seen *as* a battlefield or *as* a problem of logistics. The region itself has been overpowered. In the same way, the text, in serving the critic, is forced to submit itself to him and to his terms of reference, terms which have been set up in advance in both time and logic. In the process of conservation, the critic, however modern and original his method, is himself conserved along with it. In his profound and concerned concentration on method, he himself, as he whose method it is, becomes a mere corollary to a process—a servant. In the very process of mastering a text by revealing as conservation, the critic is left as servant. Thus, in conserving, the critic already finds himself within the realm of serving, a realm which he can never subsequently enter and take up a relationship to.

So the most important thought for the critic—how he can take up a relationship to the realm of serving—is not asked by questioning the essence of conserving but by holding himself in the realm where the serving which underlies conservation can be thought. This thinking is poetic thinking—poiesis. It is, perhaps, not so ironic that the critic, standing as he does so close to the revealing serving which is poiesis, tends to retreat from the call of that service. At the slightest touch of the threatening material with which he is dealing, the demand of the serving which underlies it opens up, and what is thus open is seen as fateful, and he glances aside. Mediating between the text and himself, with the aid of a critical method, results in neither the text nor himself being served; rather, both are used. He encounters neither the text nor himself. Instead of responding to the service contained in the realm of conserving which is opened up to him in his contact with the text, he turns aside.[4]

This move from service to mastery lies at the core of criticism as technology and is the greatest peril for the critic. The critic who turns aside denies himself the very thing that drew him to the poem in the first place. So long as the poem is not just another text to be put to use, to be submitted to a method, so long as it remains that which draws the critic to his task, then it is in control and anything may happen. The critic's mastery is at risk. Conserving is out of the question. The poem reserves itself to itself and the critic along with it. Here, knowing is no longer at the service of doing but re-asserts itself through submission. This move from mastery to submission is critical for the critic. The critical moment (in, for instance, the course of an illness) is when things may go either one way or the other. Critique is a scepticism in the face of judgement, a return to the openness which lies within the quest before it is converted into a question. It is in this conversion that the critic comes down on one side or the other, that the fundamental move is made and the genuine dialectical openness of scepticism may be lost. Only within this openness is it more difficult to ask the question than to answer it. Indeed, the distinction between the genuine and the false can be located here. The critic who questions in order to produce an answer will always find asking the question easy, whereas the critic who questions because he is truly on a quest will not.[5]

The genuine critic will recognise the essential lack at the heart of his quest. He will recognise that he does not know and that any question that directs itself towards an answer comes after the response that it pretends to await. On the other hand, the question of a genuine quest leaves the answer open. The question still comes after but in an entirely different way. As the answer is not now predetermined but undetermined, it presents itself as truly questionable. The question of the genuine quest is drawn on by the openness of what is questioned. The poem—the answer—is prior to all questioning and is known in a quite definite way. It is this knowledge that draws the question from us. It is the pretext for our question. The question about the text can be derived only from the text and should return the text to us. If it fails to do this, then the text has been ignored in some way and has drawn forth an inappropriate question which will distort the answer. Thus the relationship of question and answer is reversed: the voice that speaks to us from the past is asking a question of us, placing the way we understand ourselves in the open and, by so doing, destroys any possible 'objectivity', as it does any possible 'subjectivity'. It is each of us as critic that must re-assemble the question to which the text is the answer.

In provoking our questioning the text opens up our world as that part of it that stands out from the past. The critic is not the poet, and his reading of the text must accept the loss that this implies and renounce that which is lost. Only by so doing can this loss itself be what it is—a loss. This knowledge, that there are dimensions of the text which underlie what he can grasp, implies for him a continual renunciation which lies at the heart of the critical experience. It is a renunciation which is tempting to bypass—a temptation which we can see typified in the auction rooms where high prices are paid for possession of the original document, for the authorised signature. The 'original' does not in some way contain the origin of the text. The words of the text do not refer back to some fixed and closed moment in the past when they were set down in their final form, but forward to the critic who reads them now. All texts are essentially anonymous in that they are detached from the circumstances of their composition. The origin of their power lies in the words themselves. It is the power of the poem as answer that draws the question from the critic.

Thus the critic is not the master of a collection of pieces of linguistic information but is in the service of the text which reserves itself for him and does so by disrupting his desire to be at home in existence, forcing him into 'uncertainties, Mysteries, doubts'[6] and so along the path of the quest. This quest, in which the answer opens itself towards the possibility of a question and sustains itself within the open thus created, is the critical experience that renounces the conclusive answer. In this way, the critic renounces his mastery over the question and, along with it, the critical language in which it is spoken.

LANGUAGE

In the con-serving of the poetic text the critic exposes the poem through the medium of language. The words of the poem are transported into the language of the chosen critical method. Along with the method, language acts as an instrument used to provide information about the poem; it is a signifier which remains in-between, reaching out to each in turn. The point at which the two commune is identified in the meaning of their communication. It is here that their meaning is enunciated. The text which activates the communion in the first place can always restate it. But language as the in-between of two human beings does not create a relationship which was not already there. The world common to each was there in the first place and persists in language which cannot then be added to it.

Existence flows through language which discloses its possibilities.[7] The separate elements which go to make up this totality can indeed be articulated in language, can be broken up into separate articles and isolated from their relationships, but only to dissolve back again into their pre-reflexive unity. This isolated data only has meaning as that which has been isolated. In this isolation, it does not first lose its world and then regain it but at all times carries its world along with it. Even the most trite and obvious of statements is not worldless. Indeed, it can only be verified by reference to the background from which it springs.[8] It cannot be considered either 'correct' or 'incorrect' if this reference cannot be made. Even language itself, for the most part, remains as background and stays dissolved in the world of which it is a part. As long as language freely grants itself to us, it refuses to isolate itself from its background and present itself overtly for our consideration. This does not mean that language is not experienced. It is, and in a quite definite way, yet without bringing itself to our attention as something experienced. Just so long as we are at home in it, language, like the world, is experienced as freely granted, bringing itself into use easily and fluently. It is 'taken for granted'. Again, like the world, language only presents itself to us to be overtly experienced—to be dealt with—when it no longer freely grants itself but draws back and withholds itself.[9] The grant of language is the flow of the vernacular in which we live, but this flow can be broken when language thrusts itself forward as something to be dealt with. The translator lives in the realm of this intrusive language all the time. For him, the word is always returning for further consideration. It may eventually settle down into the vernacular but its paternity is foreign. Varro noted just this in one of the categories of his *De Lingua Latina*. He says of language that 'there are three kinds, one vernacular born here among us; the second coming from abroad; the third hybrid born here of foreign paternity'.[10] It is vernacular language that subsumes itself to common use 'not merely for poets but for almost all of those who speak in prose'.[11] The vernacular is the language in which we feel at home, to which we are slaves and which we deserve. The language 'coming from abroad' and pilgrim language—'born here of foreign paternity'—on the other hand, always draw attention to themselves and their context either as meaningless or as strange, either as something needing translation or as something needing to be incorporated into the vernacular. By using the vernacular, we serve it. As with the world, we are thrown into its flow without first being asked, and only death can part us from it. This is the root from which our understanding of existence grows. The fluency of the vernacular which we serve enables us to say 'I am', and each particular 'I am' is rooted in the vernacular. De Nebrija says just this in the dedication to Queen Isabel of Castile in his *Gramatica Castellana* of 1493.[12] He stresses the importance of his work on grammar by emphasising to her that Castellano, the language of the conqueror, must on no account remain a pilgrim language in her new conquests in the Americas but should, as rapidly as possible, become the vernacular.

Yet this ability of language to draw attention to itself, to seem strange and to cause discomfort, to refuse to grant itself freely and without objection—the pilgrim word in the midst of the vernacular—points to a more profound relation to language, to the word which draws attention to itself not by thrusting itself forward but by doing exactly the reverse; that is, by withdrawing and refusing itself. This refusal of the word causes language itself to obtrude and make itself visible.[13] The surrounding phrases from which the word has fallen away force themselves to our attention as unable to serve us. This hiatus in speech, this disappearance of language, by disrupting its serviceability, draws our attention to it. When the word is missing, the context from which it is missing comes to the fore but always as obtrusive, as something broken apart, something servered. We can respond to this break in the flow of our vernacular in one of two ways: either by repairing the break or by accepting the break itself as the most valuable gift that language has to offer. In the first case, we in fact treat the word which has denied itself as if it were foreign and search around for a new word or phrase which might do as well. We find an equivalent in the vernacular and slot it into the gap left by the missing word. The vital withdrawal of the word which is missing is thus never faced. In searching for an alternative we turn away from the break and only turn again to face it when we have an alternative and the threat has been overcome.

But, as already suggested, this withdrawal of language is itself the greatest gift that language has to offer, and it is this gift, refused by the translator, refused in the process of replacing the missing word with an alternative, that the poet faces. 'The process of doing a translation is the exact opposite of work on original verse'.[14] The poet accepts gratefully the hint which language grants him in its withdrawal and, turning towards the hiatus thus given him, maintains himself within it. Refusing to accept any alternative, he recognises the fact (exactly the reverse of what is generally thought true of the poet) that, far from being a particularly gifted user of language—the one who, above all else, has language under his control—it is language that controls him. The poet does not use language but is its servant.[15] This renunciation of his control over language is, for the poet, a bringing to presence of language—an experiencing of language as what it is, as that which can grant itself or withhold itself. Only in renunciation can the word withhold itself. This bringing into experience (*nuntiare*) is the grant of language, not as pronouncement but as the experience of the poet.

Renunciation is not a refusal, nor is it simply an acceptance of loss. It is the bringing of a message (*nuntiare*) through a going back (*re*), and this lies at the heart of any experience. Experience is an *ex-parior*, an *ex-paraou*, a passing through or *porros*, passage. Experience is not merely involvement in an event, nor is it a collection of events into a 'life's experience'; and yet, when the word is used in this way it is not totally misused. The sort of event which is an experience stands out from the everyday background of life, because it is in some sense a dislocation of normality, a break in routine. This event is seen as a break exactly because of the return to normality, because the dislocation has been repaired. Once the disturbance is over everything becomes more or less as it was before.

Yet much lies hidden in this 'more or less'. The *ex-parior* is not a mere passing back. The two sides of the dislocation are not re-located so that the join is invisible. The *ex-parior* is a passing through which leads back, but the *parior* is a *porta* or portcullis through which the passage takes us. There is no going back as if the path had never been trodden. Even analytic investigation understands this and refers itself back in terms of its passage. For analysis, the dislocation opens up the possibility of discovering what lies behind, but the reference back is always made in terms of the discovery. The investigator speaks of the normal case in terms of his investigation. The path he has taken governs his understanding. He is unable to return to the same point. His understanding of the normal case is governed by the path which he takes to his discovery.

In this sense, all experience is 'out of the ordinary', is on a pilgrimage. The discoveries made during their passage compel a reassessment of the normal case, a reassessment which we may want to ignore. Yet this desire to ignore what has taken place implies that something *has* taken place. The normal case has been transformed by the experience. The significance in this for us lies in the possibility of our refusing to ignore it. The passage through which we pass back is opened up for us in such a way that it retains itself in its very return. The world which we are after our passing through the portal of experience has been re-allocated, and experience is this continual re-allocation. Experience re-allocates our world to us in such a way that it preserves it as that which is to come.[16] In this way the poet recalls experience to our attention; he re-allocates experience to us. He re-collects experience not as something finished with but as projection. This re-allocation is a gathering together which grants itself to the poet and, through him, to us. This gathering together is a preservation which preserves itself of its own accord. It is in this way that renunciation is the bringing of a message through a going back to—a re-collection of —the origin. Only that which withdraws into itself can grant itself as that which withdraws, as that which it *is*. The poet is released into the nearness of that which withdraws in a time of misery, and it is this release which governs the re-allocation. In this experience language is preserved for him as that which is to come. Our experience with language transforms our relation to language.[17]

The experience of the poet is of a critical kind, for it is he who, in renunciation, renounces not only the word but the experience of which it is the word. When the word withdraws itself, the thing that it announces vanishes along with it. Unlike the translator, the poet refuses to retain the word's meaning in the expectation of filling the hiatus left by the withdrawal of the word. For him, another word will not do as well. For him, the being of the word withdraws along with the word for its being. The two deny themselves simultaneously because they grant themselves simultaneously. What withdraws is the word for the word and the being of language along with it. The withdrawal of the word for being and withdrawal of the being of the word are simultaneous for the poet and reveal themselves in his experience of the withdrawal of the word for the word. The poet's renunciation reveals the being of language which is brought to language within the renunciation.

The poet's experience with language is the property of the poet and the ground for our assertive demand on language that it correctly express the visible world. Language can only be 'correct' in this way if we turn aside from the experience, and this is something which the poet, by his very nature, cannot do. Experience can only be expressed 'correctly' when it deals with the normal case, when a dislocation in the flow of experience—the *ex-parior*—either refuses itself or is denied. This is why the aim of all assertive thinking is an objectivity which implies a superficial self-sameness and continuity. It cannot cope with change unless that, too, is regular and predictable. This is not and never can be the language of experience, because it turns away from experience and judges only the normal case. The critic, too, when he writes about the language of the poem is not dealing with the language of experience, because he turns away from the experience with language. He denies the dislocation which allows a re-allocation and, by so doing, he denies his experience with language, the experience that language withdraws itself. Only thus can he write *about* the poem.

Assertive thinking is the reverse of poetic thinking. One assaults language, while the other renounces it. One demands that language reveal, the other accepts that what language reveals of itself is a shyness of revelation—a love of withdrawal. Demands are made of one that serves and assertive thought takes language as servant. Renunciation accepts the reverse—that it is we who serve language and that its revelation lies within its gift. The poet, by renouncing the word, by letting it withdraw apart, releases himself into the *parior* along which the word also passes and, by so doing, arrives at a nearness to language in which it can grant itself as the poet's own, in which it can gather itself together—re-collect itself—in a re-allocation.

The critic is on a pilgrimage between the vernacular and the foreign. His passage lies in the land of the poetic vernacular, and yet he carries with him the load of his foreign tongue. His experience of the poem is the experience of a pilgrim, which is to say that this pilgrimage (his *peregrinum*) is a passage through a foreign land, which he experiences as a passing through (as *ex-parior*). The source of this pilgrimage, his experience, is a renunciation which follows the poetic vernacular in its withdrawal, but not as some linear passage to some final point. The critic's is an *ex-parior* of language, the source of which lies in its very nature—that it withdraws itself. The poem opens up this experience for him, and he retains himself within it. His pilgrimage is a re-collection which thinks of the source as the experience of the pilgrimage, but only as that experience of which the source is the poem. The pilgrim bears the source along with him on the pilgrimage and bears the pilgrimage back to the source.

For the pilgrim who is critic, language is pilgrim—'born here of foreign paternity'—both given birth in his renunciation and born along by it. His renunciation is a bringing of a message by a re-turn to this source. This re-turn is a continual re-nunciation of any translation of the poem into the foreign language which he bears along with him. It is not a return to any particular critical method, but a re-turn to the source—to the poetic text. At the same time it is a re-turn to the dis-location which gave birth to the pilgrimage, which is again the poetic text itself. For him, then, language is always on the move, on a pilgrimage, is always re-turning to itself in a continual re-nunciation of its power over the poem. Also, it is re-nouncing the vernacular of the poem whose power it feels, because this power moves the text in a constant denial and removal. This constant re-moving and re-turning is the life of the critic who exists in the shadow of the poem and is always drawn on again in the wake of the movement of language,

which is a re-moval into the opening of which language itself is the
source. The critic is not the poet, and his language is not the language
of the poem but is 'born here of foreign paternity'. The source of what
he shows is the poetic text, both as what he seeks and as what sets him
on his way. What he says must always be in shadow and superfluous,
but the shadow is that cast by the poem, and the reader who follows
the critic into the poem's shadow follows him there in the wake of
language, the experience of which, in the first instance, is the source of
the poem.

THE POEM

That which is preserved by the critic is that which the poem reserves to
itself. Normally, that which is of service to us is not ob-served but used
automatically and without conscious thought. Our attention is, for the
most part, in advance of what we use, ahead of the action we take to
achieve our purpose. We use things in order to produce a result, and so
long as they adequately serve us, they remain in the background. This
situation changes dramatically when the thing fails in its service.
Isolated from its background, it then presents itself to us as a problem;
it throws itself in front of us as an obstacle to our orderly progress.
This *ob-jectum*, thrown down as ob-stacle, presents itself for observation. The threat produced in this way has to be overcome, to be
set right and placed back into service.

The poem also forces itself to our attention, and yet in this case there
is a difference. We attend to the poem not because of some fault but
because of its very perfection; not because of something temporary but
because of its permanent and eternal quality.

In what sense is it possible to say that our experience of the thing as
temporarily faulty and our experience of the poetic text as permanent
and perfect are related? Is it only in the sense that they are both
experienced, in the sense that each represents itself to conscious-
ness—or is it in our reaction to any such presentation? When the tool
presents itself to us through a dis-location in its service, our feeling of
being at home in a set of involvements in which the tool figures is
threatened. That threat can only be rectified by a reintegration of the
tool back into its involvements—by our putting it back into service
again. We do this by attending to the fault.[18] When the poem presents

itself to us, it too can do so as a dis-location in its mere serviceability. The poem, the work of art, is no longer merely pleasant, no longer merely calms us down after a hard day's work, but instead opens up a threat to the calm continuity of our prospects. The poem, like the tool, dis-locates the pre-reflexive certainty of our day-to-day existence and dis-rupts it, throwing up alternative possibilities which we would, perhaps, rather ignore.

In the same way as, for the most part, we turn away from the possibilities opened up by the discontinuity of involvements in the case of the faulty tool, we ignore the possibilities presented to us by the poetic text. The possibilities closest to us can be opened up in each of these cases, and usually the response is to correct the dis-location and to re-establish the case as it was prior to the dis-ruption. This is done by observation and correction: the tool is repaired, the poem is placed under the certainty of a critical method. Each is explained and understood, and in this way our superiority over against the threat is re-established.

Yet the distinction between the tool and the poetic text remains. We are so accustomed to explaining and correcting dis-ruptions that we automatically treat every threat in the same way and fail to notice that, whereas this method repairs the broken tool to its former state, the poem is altered—whereas the tool becomes itself again, the poem becomes something else, and that this is the very secret of its permanence and immortality. Both repaired tool and explained poem reintegrate themselves once again into the pre-reflexive background of experience. But, in order for this to take place, the method must be at the service of the tool and be used to pre-serve it, while the poem must be forced into the service of the method and used to con-serve it. The method falls away from the pre-served tool once it has served its purpose whereas, in the case of the poem, it is the poem that falls away from the method and the method that is retained. This must be, as noted earlier, because the tool dis-locates experience only when faulty—only when it can no longer perform its function—while the poem dis-locates when perfect, when it can best perform its function. While explanation puts the tool back into serviceability, it destroys the serviceability of the poem.

Thus the poetic text is the reverse of the tool. Its serviceability lies in the experience of dis-location which it grants us, and thus any approach to the poetic text that takes advantage of its nature must let the dis-location be. It is the experience of the open itself which is of value and that avoids a re-turn or re-location of the normal case and encourages a re-allocation which incorporates the experience which has been passed through.

What then is the critic to do? In order to save what is of value in the poem, in order to be true to the very natue of the poem, it seems that he must make his comments superfluous. Any explanation or adjustment of the text will tend to 'put it to rights' and act as its replacement. If the nature of the poem is to be retained and, more than that, allowed to reveal itself with ever greater intensity, then critical discourse must each time destroy itself in its own effort, must each time retreat in the face of the poetic revelation of the poem. Such self-effacing discourse must add nothing to the poem either by drawing attention to itself or by drawing attention to the poem. It must absent itself as, at the same time, it reveals absence in the poem. The aim of critical discourse is to vanish, taking the critic along with it, in favour of the poem—to make itself superfluous in respect of an absence which lies at the heart of the poem. Critical discourse must let this absence be and, at the same time, must fall away in the face of it. The nature of critical discourse must attune itself to the nature of the poem, each re-turning into itself. Critical thought must pre-serve rather than con-serve; or rather, it must allow the poem to reserve itself to itself. In other words, it must think poetically. This poetical thinking is a standing within a clearing opened up by the spell of words, a spell which the critic, like the poet, must avoid breaking up by an assault over the gap. The nearness of poetry and poetical thinking must be respected, not bridged.

The critic must give up e-nunciation in favour re-nunciation. Re-nunciation is the bringing of a message by virtue of a return. In this way the poetic message is allowed to re-serve itself—to return to itself, to keep itself in reserve—and the critic pre-serves it.

How is this to be done? If the critic is not merely the wielder of a methodology for which any text will do equally well, if he is drawn into the experience opened up by the poem, if the poem acts as the source of his journey through the dis-ruption of the day-to-day continuity of habit, then the path he travels is not the secure one to which he is accustomed. The poem opens up for him the possibility of travelling a new path for which the old signposts are no longer of any use. The critic takes this path away from home and into a foreign country. The language he brings with him is of no use here, for in the poetic landscape dwell the poets who are born along in a vernacular which he can only 'understand' by translation into the foreign critical language the traveller has now left behind him. Equally, he is unable to speak the poetic vernacular. He is born along by the poem into the realm opened up by the vernacular, in which the vernacular comes to speech in such a way that translation is denied him without his returning whence he came. He is a pilgrim, a *pere-grinum*, one that is on a journey. He is *per-ager*, one who takes a path through a field, country or land. On this path his language is pilgrim—'it is born here of foreign paternity'. 'Born' is here 'a carrying along' as well as 'a giving birth'. The language of the traveller is 'born' here in both these ways, which are nothing other than the same way. His pilgrimage was given birth by the poem for it was the poem that set him on his way. He is also born along by what he seeks which is, once again, the poem. He is born along by the poem which is the source of his pilgrimage and is what he seeks on his pilgrimage. If he merely seeks out what he seeks by an assault upon it, if he carries with him the apparatus—the critical language—with which to do it, he remains exactly where he was and drags the source—the poem—to him, thus closing off the path between himself and the poem by ignoring; by turning aside from; its nature as that which beckons. He has to resort to a mere translation of the text into his own foreign language, ignoring the call of the vernacular to a pilgrimage.

Thus, if he accepts the call, he must not seek out what he seeks but renounce it and, in so doing, re-turn to what set him on his way. Re-nunciation is a bringing of a message through a going back to the source and never the taking of a particular message to that source. The path is not *to* the source in order to arrive there and present it with a message, but rather a pilgrimage back (*re*) along the path to the origin of the pilgrimage. Experiencing this pilgrimage, the critic enters the realm opened up for him by the withdrawal of language. In effect, what he seeks is nothing other than this opening up, which is the lack of language which he, following the poet, experiences. This is the origin to which he re-turns; that is, once again, the poem. Re-nouncing language, the critic is taken along the path of what with-draws—language itself—allowing it, in its withdrawal, to be just what it *is*. In its withdrawal, the source brings its message to him or has already brought it. This message is ex-pressed in the language of the pilgrim, a language which he has brought with him, a language 'born here of foreign paternity', a language given birth here and, at the same time, carried here, a language which springs from the pilgrimage opened up by the poem. The message is born to the clearing, thus opened up and born *in* it.

Once on a pilgrimage and remaining true to the source of the pilgrimage, the pilgrim can no more transform his experience of it back into an inappropriate form as he can form that experience into the vernacular of the poet, because he lacks the poet's gift—the grant of the vernacular. In order to bear the message, he must renounce both. He must renounce his foreign language as inappropriate to the pilgrimage and also renounce the vernacular which is given to the poet. In this dual renunciation he will be granted the poet's message, for his pilgrimage has its source in the poem; and the language of his message is pilgrim also. His pilgrimage to the source, in order to be what it is—a pilgrimage—must maintain itself in the call of the poem. For this to occur, the poem must re-serve itself for the critic and, in so doing, remain that which calls—remain, that is, near-by in the critic's neighbourhood, but other. The pilgrim language speaks of that which withdraws itself and which, in its very withdrawal calls the pilgrim to his pilgrimage, draws him on to the source of his journey. This is the critical experience. The poetic text, the source of his pilgrimage, withdraws itself, and it is this withdrawal that is the message, and it is a source that, by its very nature can never be found, discovered or brought into the clear light of day.

The critic's message is none other than his pilgrimage to this source, and it is thus a piligrimage of renunciation. Maintaining himself on this pilgrimage is the critic's task.

Notes and Abbreviations

ABBREVIATIONS

Keats' Poems

References to Keats' poems have been made to the following four editions:

HEd—Hampstead Edition	H. Buxton Forman (ed.), *The Poetical Works and Other Writings of John Keats* (New York, Phaeton Press, 1970).
Ox—Oxford English Texts	H.W. Garrod (ed.), *John Keats: Poetical Works* (London, Oxford University Press, 1956).
OSA—Oxford Standard Authors	H.W. Garrod (ed.), *The Poetical Works of John Keats* (London, Oxford University Press, 1956).
AEP—Anotated English Poets	Miriam Arlott (ed.), *The Poems of John Keats*, (London, Longman, 1957)

Each reference has been preceded by the name of the poem and the line numbers of the quotation. The abbreviations used are listed below with the page numbers of the poem in each of the four editions.

		HEd	Ox	AEP	OSA
Agnes	— The Eve of St Agnes	3:91	236	450	195
Calidore	— Calidore	1:29	14	36	11
Clarke	— Epistle to Charles Cowden Clarke	1:63	35	54	29
Elgin	— On Seeing the Elgin Marbles	4:44	478	104	376
End	— Endymion	2:1	63	116	153
Fall of H	— Fall of Hyperion—A Dream	3:255	509	655	401
Full Many	— Epistle to my Brother George —Full Many a Dreary Hour	1:57	31	49	25
Great Spirits	— Addressed to Haydon II	1:91	48	67	39
Grec	— Ode on a Grecian Urn	3:153	260	532	209

Haydon	— Addressed to Haydon I	1:90	47	66	39
Hyp	— Hyperion	3:187	276	394	221
Ind	— Ode on Indolence	4:189	447	541	355
Induction	— Specimen of an Induction to a Poem	1:25	12	33	9
Isa	— Isabella or The Pot of Basil	3:53	215	326	179
I Stood	— I stood tip-toe upon a little hill	1:9	3	85	3
Lamia	— Lamia	3:9	191	613	161
Lear	— On Sitting Down to Read 'King Lear' Once Again	4:76	483	295	380
Mathew	— Epistle to George Felton Mathew	1:53	28	24	23
Melan	— Ode on Melancholy	3:184	274	538	219
Milton	— Ode: On Seeing a Lock of Milton's Hair	4:72	479	292	377
Night	— Ode to a Nightingale	3:145	257	523	207
Otho	— Otho the Great	5:7	309	544	247
Psyche	— Ode to Psyche	3:159	262	514	311
Reynolds	— Epistle to J.H. Reynolds Esq.	4:133	484	320	381
Sleep	— Sleep and Poetry	1:91	51	69	42
Thrush	— What the Thrush Said	4:89	482	351	367
Tomb	— Sonnet: On Visiting the Tomb of Burns	4:123	489	357	385
Why Did	— Sonnet: Why did I laugh tonight?	4:193	470	488	370

This book is not, for the most part, concerned with details of punctuation and orthography, thus, except where specifically stated, all quotations follow Garrod as being the standard text. Any doubts as to textual details may be resolved by reference to his excellent annotations, to which Miriam Arlott has made some useful additions.

Keats' Letters

References to the letters have been made to the following three editions:

HEd—Hampstead Edition	H. Buxton Forman (ed.), *The Poetical Works and Other Writings of John Keats* (New York, Phaeton Press, 1970).
R.—Rollins	H.E. Rollins (ed.), *The Letters of John Keats* (Cambridge, Cambridge University Press, 1958).
P.—Page	F. Page (ed.), *Letters of John Keats*, Worlds Classics (London, Oxford University Press, 1965).

Each of Keats' letters carries a kind of Opus number. I have used the accepted number to precede each reference and this is followed by the name of his correspondent and the date of the letter. H.E. Rollins includes letters *to* Keats in his edition and the numbers he uses have been added in brackets after his page numbers. All quotations have followed Rollins and any doubts as to textual detail may usually, at least in the first instance, be resolved by reference to his notes.

Poems Included in Letters

Where a Keats poem appears in one of his letters, reference has only been made to the editions of the poems. Below is a list of the page numbers in the above editions of the letters where a poem used in this book is included in a letter.

		HEd	R.	P.
Full Many	— L.2 to George Keats, –. 8.1816	6:6	1:105(5)	—
Great Spirits	— L.5 to Benjamin Robert Haydon, 20.11.1816	6:13	1:118(12)	2
Lear	— L.41 to George and Thomas Keats, 23.1.1818	6:128	1:214(56)	—
Mathew	— L. to George Felton Mathew	—	1:100(2)	—
Milton	— L.40 to Benjamin Bailey, 23.1.1818	6:123	1:211(55)	64
Psyche	— L.123 to George and Georgiana Keats, 14.2 to 3.5.1818	7:259	2:106(159)	269
Reynolds	— L.58 to John Hamilton Reynolds, 25.3.1818	6:179	1:259(74)	95

Thrush	— L.48 to John Hamilton			
	Reynolds, 19.2.1818	6:149	1:233(62)	81
Tomb	— L.73 to Thomas Keats,			
	29.6–2.7.1818	7:39	1:308(62)	81
Why Did	— L.123 to George and			
	Georgiana Keats,			
	14.2–3.5.1818	7:290	2:80(159)	251

William Blake

References to the works of Blake have been made to two of the editions used for Keats' poems as follows

AEP—Annotated English Poets	W.H. Stevenson (ed.), *The Poems of William Blake* (London, Longman, 1971).
OSA—Oxford Standard Authors	Geoffrey Keynes (ed.), *Blake: The Complete Writings* (London, Oxford University Press, 1966).

NOTES

Chapter 1

1. John Middleton Murry, *Keats and Shakespeare*, (London, University Press, 1925) p.12.
2. Full Many 54 HEd 1:59, Ox 32, AEP 50, OSA 26.
3. HEd 1:8.
4. H.E. Rollins (ed.), *The Keats Circle: Letters and Papers 1816–1879* (Cambridge, Mass, Harvard University Press 1948), vol. 2, p. 55.
5. Clarke, Charles and Mary Cowden, *Recollections of Writers* (Fontwell, Centaur Press, 1969) p.125.
6. *See* Ch. 5.
7. L.156 to G. and G. Keats 17 to 27.9.1819, HEd 8:107, R.2:212, P.354.
8. Colvin Sidney, *John Keats: His Life and Poetry, His Friends, Critics and After-Fame* (London, Macmillan 1925) p.25.
9. Mathew 2, HEd 1:53, Ox 24, AEP 24, OSA 28.
10. George Felton Mathew, 'To a Poetical Friend', HEd 1:115.
11. *Ibid.*
12. Mathew 32—3, HEd 1:54, Ox 29, AEP 25, OSA 23–4.
13. Mathew 18, HEd 1:54, Ox 28, AEP 25, OSA 23.
14. Clarke, Charles and Mary Cowden, *Recollections of Writers* (Fontwell, Centaur Press 1969) p.132.
15. *Ibid.*

16. Leigh Hunt, 'Young Poets', *Examiner*, 21 Dec 1816.
17. Leigh Hunt, 'The Story of Rimini', London, 1816, Preface p. xiii–vi.
18. *Ibid.* p. xvi.
19. Induction 1 and 11, HEd 1:23, Ox 12, AEP 33–4, OSA 9.
20. Induction 49–52, HEd 1:27, Ox 13, AEP 35, OSA 10.
21. Induction 56–7 HEd 1:27, Ox 13, AEP 35, OSA 10.
22. Induction 62–4, HEd 1:27, Ox 13, AEP 36, OSA 10.
23. Clarke 42–8, HEd 1:64—5, Ox 36, AEP 56, OSA 30.
24. Calidore 109, HEd 1:33, Ox 16, AEP 41, OSA 13.
25. Calidore 77, HEd 1:332, Ox 16, AEP 40, OSA 13.
26. Calidore 116, HEd 1:33, Ox 17, AEP 41, OSA 13.
27. Calidore 127–8, HEd 1:33, Ox 17, AEP 41, OSA 14.
28. Full Many 72–3, HEd 1:60, Ox 33, AEP 51, OSA 27.
29. Full Many 73–83, HEd 1:60, Ox 33, AEP 51–2, OSA 27.
30. Haydon 11, HEd 1:90, Ox 47, AEP 67, OSA 39.
31. Leigh Hunt, Sonnet: 'To Benjamin Haydon', AEP note, p.68.
32. Haydon 13–14, HEd 1:90, Ox 47, AEP 67, OSA 39.
33. L.3 to Charles Cowden Clarke 31.10.1816, HEd 6:10–11 R. 1:114–5(8), P.2.
34. Great Spirits 7–8 and 11–12, HEd 1:91, Ox 48, AEP 68, OSA 39.
35. Jack Stillinger, *The Letters of Charles Armitage Brown* (Cambridge, Mass, Harvard University Press, 1966) p.316.
36. W.B. Pope, (ed.) *The Diary of Benjamin Robert Haydon 1816–24* (Cambridge, Mass, Harvard University Press 1960) p.101.
37. *Ibid.*
38. Elgin 5, HEd 4:44, Ox 478, AEP 104, OSA 376.
39. Elgin 4, HEd 4:44, Ox 478, AEP 104, OSA 376.
40. Sharp, William, *The Life and Letters of Joseph Severn* (London, Sampson, Low, Marston & Co, 1892) p.29.
41. Sleep 66–7, HEd 1:101, Ox 52–3, AEP 72, OSA 43.
42. Sleep 10, HEd 1:101, Ox51, AEP 72, OSA 44.
43. Sleep 10, HEd 1:99, Ox 51, AEP 70, OSA 42.
44. Sleep 101–2, HEd 1:102, Ox 53, AEP 73, OSA 44.
45. *Ibid.*
46. Sleep 123–5, HEd 1:103, Ox 54, AEP 74, OSA 45.
47. Sleep 102–4, HEd 1:102, Ox 53, AEP 73–4, OSA 44.
48. Sleep 122, HEd 1:103, Ox 54, AEP 74, OSA 45.
49. Sleep 124–5, HEd 1:103, Ox 54, AEP 74, OSA 45.
50. Sleep 151–3, HEd 1:104, Ox 55, AEP 76, OSA 45–6.
51. Sleep 127, HEd 1:103, Ox 54, AEP 75, OSA 45.
52. Sleep 153–4, HEd 1:104, Ox 54, AEP 76, OSA 46.
53. Sleep 156–7, HEd 1:104, Ox 54, AEP 76, OSA 46.
54. Sleep 157–8, HEd 1:104, Ox 54, AEP 76, OSA 46.
55. Sleep 159–62, HEd 1:104, Ox 54, AEP 76, OSA 46.

56. Sleep 163–5, HEd 1:104, Ox 55, AEP 76, OSA 46.
57. Sleep 193–4, HEd 1:105, Ox 56, AEP 77, OSA 47.
58. Sleep 194–7 and 199–200, HEd 1:105, Ox 56, AEP 77, OSA 47.
59. Sleep 230–1, HEd 1:106, Ox 57, AEP 79, OSA 48.
60. Sleep 232–3, HEd 1:106, Ox 57, AEP 79, OSA 48.
61. Sleep 233–5, HEd 1:106, Ox 57, AEP 79, OSA 48.
62. Sleep 241–2, HEd 1:106–7, Ox 57, AEP 79, OSA 48.
63. Sleep 235–40, HEd 1:106, Ox 57, AEP 79, OSA 48.
64. Sleep 245–7, HEd 1:107, Ox 57, AEP 80, OSA 48.
65. Sleep 267–8, HEd 1:107, Ox 58, AEP 80–1, OSA 48.
66. Sleep 265–6, HEd 1:107, Ox 58, AEP 80, OSA 48.
67. Murry, *Keats and Shakespeare*, p. 23.
68. Sleep 270–3, HEd 1:108, Ox 58, AEP 81, OSA 49.
69. Sleep 275–6, HEd 1:108, Ox 58, AEP 81, OSA 49.
70. Sleep 282–3, HEd 1:108, Ox 58, AEP 81, OSA 49.
71. Sleep 284–8, HEd 1:108, Ox 58, AEP 81, OSA 49.
72. Sleep 289–91, HEd 1:108, Ox 58, AEP 81, OSA 49.
73. Sleep 291–4, HEd 1:108, Ox 58, AEP 81, OSA 49.
74. Sleep 306, HEd 1:109, Ox 59, AEP 82, OSA 49.
75. Sleep 307, HEd 1:109, Ox 59, AEP 82, OSA 49.
76. Sleep 307–10, HEd 1:109, Ox 59, AEP 82, OSA 49.
77. I Stood 121, HEd 1:17, Ox 7, AEP 91, OSA 6.
78. I Stood 123–6, HEd 1:17, Ox 7, AEP 94, OSA 6.
79. I Stood 116, HEd 1:17, Ox 7, AEP 90, OSA 6.
80. I Stood 186–7, HEd 1:21, Ox 9, AEP 94, OSA 7.
81. I Stood 191, HEd 1:21, Ox 10, AEP 94, OSA 7.
82. I Stood 192, HEd 1:21, Ox 10, AEP 95, OSA 8.
83. I Stood 193, HEd 1:21, Ox 10, AEP 95, OSA 8.
84. I Stood 197, HEd 1:21, Ox 10, AEP 95, OSA 8.
85. I Stood 201–4, HEd 1:21, Ox 10, AEP 95, OSA 8.
86. I Stood 209–10, HEd 1:22, Ox 10, AEP 95, OSA 8.
87. I Stood 239–41, HEd 1:24, Ox 11, AEP 96, OSA 9.
88. I Stood 242, HEd 1:24, Ox 11, AEP 96, OSA 9.

Chapter 2

1. L. 2 to Charles Cowden Clarke 9.10.1816, HEd 6:4, R. 1:113(7), P. 1.
2. L. 41 to George and Thomas Keats 23.1.1818, HEd 6:128, R. 1:214(56), P. 67.
3. L. 40 to Benjamin Bailey 23.1.1818, HEd 6:123, R. 1:211(55), P. 64.
4. L. 55 to Benjamin Robert Haydon 14.3.1818, HEd 6:168, R. 1:250(70) P.–.
5. L. 44 to John Hamilton Reynolds 3.2.1818, HEd 6:141 R. 1:255(59) P. 75.

6. L. 43 to Reynolds 31.1.1818, HEd 6:133, R. 1:219(58). P.–
7. L.25 to Bailey 8.10.1817, HEd 6:76, R. 1: 170(38), P. 36.
8. Rejected Preface to 'Endymion', HEd 2:13.
9. L. 15 to Haydon 10.5.1817, HEd 6:41–2, R. 1:141–2(26), P. 14–15.
10. L. 19 to Fanny Keats 10.9.1817, HEd 6:54, R. 1:154(32), P.22.
11. Rejected Preface to 'Endymion', HEd 2:14.
12. L. 25 to Bailey 8.10.1817, HEd 6:76, R. 1:170(38), P. 35–6.
13. L. 25 to Bailey 8.10.1817, HEd 6:76, R. 1:169–70(38), P. 36.
14. L. 14 to Leigh Hunt 10.5.1817, HEd 6:36, R. 1:139(25), P. 12.
15. L. 15 to Haydon 10 to 11.5.1817, HEd 6:41, R. 1:141(26), P. 14—quotes
Shakespeare: *King Lear* IV.vi.16.
16. L. 25 to Bailey 8.10.1817, HEd 6:76, R. 1:170(38), P. 36.
17. L. 15 to Haydon 10 to 11.5.1817, HEd 6:41, R. 1:141(26), P. 14.
18. L. 25 to Bailey 8.10.1817, HEd 6:75, R. 1:169(38), P. 35.
19. End 1:22, HEd 2:22, Ox 65, AEP 121, OSA 55.
20. End 1:39,41,45–7,55,57, HEd 2:23–4, Ox 66, AEP 122, OSA 56.
21. L. 14 to Hunt 10.5.1817, HEd 6:36, R. 1:139 (25), P. 12.
22. L. 14 to Hunt 10.5.1817, HEd 6:36–7, R. 1:139(25), P. 12–13.
23. L. 15 to Haydon 10.11.1817, HEd 6:41, R. 1:141(26), P. 14.
24. L. 15 to Haydon HEd 6:42, R. 1:142(26), P. 15.
25. L. 16 to Taylor and Hessey 16.5.1817, HEd 6:48, R. 1:146(27), P. 19.
26. L. 19 to Fanny Keats 10.9.1817, HEd 6:54–6, R. 1:154(32), P. 22–3.
27. Bailey quoted by Lord Houghton, HEd 6:54.
28. L. 22 to Reynolds 21.9.1817, HEd 6:69, R. 1:166(36), P. 31.
29. L. 24 to Haydon 28.9.1817, HEd 6:73, R. 1:167–8(37), P. 33–4.
30. L. 24 to Haydon 28.9.1817, HEd 6:73 R. 1:168(37), P. 34.
31. L. 26 to Bailey 30.10.1817, HEd 6:78, R. 1:172(39), P. 38.
32. L. 26 to Bailey 30.10.1817, HEd 6:82–3, R. 1:175(39), P. 40.
33. L.31 to Bailey 22.11.1817, HEd 6:100, R. 1:187(43), P. 51.
34. The lines in each book in fact number as follows—Book I, 992; II, 1023;
III, 1032; IV, 1003.
35. Rejected Preface to 'Endymion', HEd 2:14.
36. L. 16 to Taylor and Hessey 16.5.1817, HEd 6:48, R. 1:146(27), P. 19.
37. Preface to 'Endymion', HEd 2:14.
38. Rejected Preface to 'Endymion', HEd 2:11.
39. L. 115 to Haydon 8.3.1819, HEd 7:213, R. 2:43(149), P. 220.
40. L. 25 to Bailey 8.10.1817, HEd 6:76, R. 1:169(38), P. 36.
41. Rejected Preface to 'Endymion', HEd 2:14.
42. Preface to 'Endymion', HEd 2:11.
43. L. 48 to Reynolds 19.1.1818, HEd 6.149, R. 1:232(62), P. 80.
44. L. 51 to Taylor 27.2.1818, HEd 6:151, R. 1:238–9(65), P. 84.
45. L. 51 to Taylor 27.2.1818, HEd 6:151, R. 1:238(65), P. 84.
46. L. 32 to G. and Th. Keats 21.12.1817, HEd 6:104, R. 1:194(45), P. 53.
47. L. 31 to Bailey 22.11.1817, HEd 6:97, R. 1:184(43), P. 48.

48. L. 16 to Taylor and Hessey 16.5.1817, HEd 6:48, R. 1:146(27), P. 19.
49. Preface to 'Endymion', HEd 2:11.
50. Julian Offray de la Mettrie, *Man a Machine* (La Salle, Illinois, The Open Court Publishing Co, 1953) p. 193.
51. John Locke, *An Essay Concerning Human Understanding*, P.H. Nidditch (ed.) (Oxford, Clarendon Press, 1975) Book IV, ch. 17:8, p. 680.
52. John Gregory, *A Comparative View of the State and Faculties of Man with those of the Animal World* (Dublin, 1778) p. 187.
53. August Wilhelm Von Schlegel, *Lectures on Dramatic Art and Literature*, trans J. Black (London, H.G. Bohn, 1846) Lecture 22, p. 35.
54. William Hazlitt, 'Lectures on the English Poets' in P.P. Howe (ed.), *The Complete Works* (London, Dent, 1930) vol. 5, p. 4–5.
55. Samuel Taylor Coleridge, 'On Poetry and Art, addenda to *Biographia Literaria* (London, Rest Fenner, 1817) vol 2, p. 254.
56. Hazlitt, 'English Poets' in Howe (ed.), *The Complete Works*, vol. 5, p.4.
57. *Ibid.*—quotes Shakespeare, *Cymbeline* II.ii.19–21.
58. *Ibid.*
59. Coleridge, *Biographia*, vol. 2, ch. 15, p. 16.
60. L. 31 to Bailey 22.11.1817, HEd 6:97–8, R. 1:184(43), P. 48.
61. L. 31 to Bailey 22.11.1817, HEd 6:98, R. 1:185(43), P. 49.
62. *Ibid.*
63. L. 64 to Reynolds 3.5.1818, HEd 7:9–10, R. 1:281(80), P. 116.
64. L. 64 to Reynolds 3.5.1818, HEd 7:9, R. 1:281(80), P. 115–6.
65. L. 31 to Bailey 22.11.1817, HEd 6:98, R. 1:185(43), P. 49. Italics added.
66. Hazlitt, 'English Poets' in Howe (ed.), *The Complete Works*, vol. 5, p. 4–5.
67. E.R. Dodds, *The Greeks and the Irrational* (Berkeley, University of California Press, 1951) p. 185–6.
68. L. 31 to Bailey 22.11.1817, HEd 6:98–9, R. 1:185(43), P. 49–50.
69. L. 31 to Bailey 22.11.1817, HEd 6:98, R. 1:185(43), P. 49.
70. *Ibid.*
71. End 1:777–81, HEd 2:60–1, Ox 80, AEP 154, OSA 74.
72. End 1:795–7, HEd 2:62, Ox 89, AEP 155, OSA 74.
73. End 1:296–8, HEd 2:36, Ox 73, AEP 133, OSA 62.
74. End 1:294–6, HEd 2:36, Ox 73, AEP 133, OSA 62.
75. End 1:796–800, HEd 2:62, Ox 89, AEP 155, OSA 74–5.
76. End 1:801–11, HEd 2:62, Ox 89, AEP 155–6, OSA 75.
77. End 1:832–3, HEd 2:63, Ox 90, AEP 157, OSA 75.
78. End 1:835–42, HEd 2:63, Ox 90, AEP 157, OSA 75–6.
79. End 1:851–53, HEd 2:64, Ox 90, AEP 158, OSA 76.
80. End 1:814, HEd 2:62, Ox 89, AEP 156, OSA 75.
81. End 1:832–4, HEd 2:63, Ox 90, AEP 157, OSA 75.
82. End 1:824–5, HEd 2:63, Ox 89–90, AEP 156, OSA 75.

83. L. 48 to Reynolds 19.2.1818, HEd 6:147, R. 1:231(62), P. 79.
84. L. 31 to Bailey 22.11.1817, HEd 6:100, R. 1:186(43), P. 50.
85. L. 44 to Reynolds 3.2.1818, HEd 6:137 R. 1:223–4(59), P. 72.
86. L. 32 to G. and Th. Keats 21.12.1817, HEd 6:104, R. 1:193(45), P. 53.
87. Hazlitt, 'English Poets' in Howe (ed.) *The Complete Works*, vol. 5, p. 47.
88. James and Horatio Smith, *Rejected Addresses or the New Theatrum Poetarum* (London, 1812).
89. L. 32 to G. and Th. Keats 21.12.1817, HEd 6:103, R. 1:192–3(45), P. 53.
90. L. 32 to G. and Th. Keats 21.12.1817, HEd 6:103, R. 1:193(45), P. 53.
91. *Ibid.*
92. Arthur H. Beavan, *James and Horatio Smith* (Hurst and Blackett, London, 1899) p. 134.
93. Beavan, *James and Horatio Smith*, p. 210.
94. 'On Edmund Kean as a Shakespearian Actor' in *The Champion* 21.12.1817, HEd 5:227.
95. L. 32 to G. and Th. Keats 21.12.1817, HEd 6:103, R. 1:193(45), P. 53.
96. 'On Edmund Kean as a Shakespearian Actor' in *The Champion*, 21.12.1817, HEd 5:227.
97. L.32 to G. and Th. Keats 21.12.1817, HEd 6:103, R. 1:193(45), P. 53.
98. *Ibid.*
99. L. 156 to G. and G. Keats 17 to 27.9.1819, HEd 8:108, R. 2:213(199), P. 354.
100. L. 156 to G. and G. Keats 17 to 27.9.1819, HEd 8:108, R. 2:213(199), P. 355.
101. L. 32 to G. and Th. Keats 21.12.1817, HEd 6:103–4, R. 1:193(45), P. 53.
102. L. 93 to Richard Woodhouse 27.10.1818, HEd 7:129–30, R. 1:387(118), P. 172.
103. L. 93 to Woodhouse 27.10.1818, HEd 7:129–30, R. 1:386–7(118), P. 172.
104. L. 31 to Bailey 22.11.1817, HEd 6:97, R. 1:184(43), P. 48.
105. H. Rollins, *The Keats Circle*, (Cambridge, Mass., Harvard University Press, 1948) vol. 1, p. 57–8 *also* R. 1:388–9.
106. End 4:513–48, HEd 2:210–12, Ox 174–5, AEP 266–7, OSA 145.
107. L. 31 to Bailey 22.11.1817, HEd 6:98, R. 1:184(43), P. 48.
108. End 4:344, HEd 2:202, Ox 169, AEP 260, OSA 140.
109. End 4:348, HEd 2:202, Ox 169, AEP 260, OSA 140.
110. End 4:401–2, HEd 2:204, Ox 170, AEP 262, OSA 142.
111. End 4:407, HEd 2:205, Ox 170, AEP 262, OSA 142.
112. End 4:411 and 413–5, HEd 2:205, Ox 171, AEP 262, OSA 145.
113. End 4:430, HEd 2:206, Ox 171, AEP 263, OSA 142.
114. End 4:431, HEd 2:206, Ox 171, AEP 263, OSA 142.
115. End 4:436, HEd 2:206, Ox 171, AEP 263, OSA 143.
116. L. 31 to Bailey 22.11.1817, HEd 6:98, R. 1:185(43), P. 49
117. End 4:439, HEd 2:206, Ox 171, AEP 263, OSA 143.

118. End 4:441–2, HEd 2:206, Ox 171, AEP 263, OSA 143.
119. End 4:445, HEd 2:207, Ox 172, AEP 263, OSA 143.
120. End 4:440–1, HEd 2:206, Ox 171, AEP 263, OSA 143.
121. End 4:447, HEd 2:206, Ox 172, AEP 264, OSA 143.
122. End 4:453, HEd 2:207, Ox 172, AEP 264, OSA 143.
123. End 4:445–55, HEd 2:207, Ox 172, AEP 263–4, OSA 143.
124. End 4:459–60, HEd 2:207, Ox 172, AEP 264, OSA 143.
125. End 4:460–61, HEd 2:207, Ox 172, AEP 264, OSA 143.
126. End 4:470–2, HEd 2:208, Ox 172, AEP 264, OSA 143.
127. End 4:470–80, HEd 2:208, Ox 172–3, AEP 244–5, OSA 143–4.
128. End 4:502, HEd 2:209, Ox 173, AEP 266, OSA 144.
129. End 4:507–8; 510, HEd 2:210, Ox 173, AEP 266, OSA 144.
130. End 4:512, HEd 2:210, Ox 173, AEP 266, OSA 144.
131. William Blake, 'Milton', plate 40:32–3, AEP 563, OSA 533.
132. End 4:522–3, HEd 2:210–11, Ox 174, AEP 266, OSA 145.
133. End 4:524–5, HEd 2:211, Ox 174, AEP 266–7, OSA 145.
134. End 4:543–5, HEd 2:211–12, Ox 174, AEP 267, OSA 145.
135. End 4:533, HEd 2:211, Ox 174, AEP 267, OSA 145.
136. End 4:531–2, HEd 2:211, Ox 174, AEP 267, OSA 145.
137. End 4:537–42, HEd 2:211, Ox 174, AEP 267, OSA 145.
138. L. 32 to G. and Th. Keats 21.12.1817, HEd 6:103, R. 1:192(45), P. 5.
139. L. 123 to G. and G. Keats 14.2 to 3.1819, HEd 7:255, R. 2:78–9(159), P. 247–8.
140. End 4:526, HEd 2:211, Ox 174, AEP 267, OSA 145.
141. End 2:8, HEd 4:190, Ox 448, AEP 542, OSA 355.
142. End 4:525, HEd 2:211, Ox 174, AEP 267, OSA 145.
143. End 4:643–4, HEd 2:217, Ox 177, AEP 272, OSA 148.
144. End 4:616–9, HEd 2:215, Ox 177, AEP 271, OSA 147.
145. End 4:649–51, HEd 2:217, Ox 178, AEP 272, OSA 148.
146. End 4:752, HEd 2:222, Ox 181, AEP 275, OSA 150.
147. End 4:755–7, HEd 2:222, Ox 181, AEP 275, OSA 151.
148. End 4:982–7, HEd 2:233, Ox 187, AEP 283–4, OSA 156.

Chapter 3

1. In this chapter quotations from the 'Ode on a Grecian Urn' have not been individually referenced. The ode can be found at HEd 3:153, Ox 260, AEP 532 and OSA 209.
2. This is, perhaps pressing the point. The comma is not present in the transcript, but there was some contention between Woodhouse, Taylor

and Keats himself during the preparation of the 1820 volume. It is possible that the alteration was approved, especially as Keats had earlier stated that he was 'determined never to write more without some care in that particular'. In any event, it seems to me that the presence of the word, even as an adverb qualifying 'unravish'd', brings its other sense into play.

3.   L. 93 to Richard Woodhouse 27.10.1818, HEd 7:129, R. 1:387(118), P. 172.
4.   *Ibid.*
5.   L. 93 to Woodhouse 27.10.1818, HEd 7:130, R. 1:387(118), P. 172.
6.   L. 86 to Charles Wentworth Dilke 20 to 21.9.1818, HEd 7:114, R. 1:368-9(107), P. 166-7.
7.   L. 93 to Woodhouse 27.10.1818, HEd 7:129-30, R. 1:386-7(118), P. 172.
8.   L. 93 to Woodhouse 27.10.1818, HEd 7:129, R. 1:387(118), P. 172.
9.   L. 93 to Woodhouse 27.10.1818, HEd 7:130, R.1:387(118), P. 172.
10. L. 86 to Dilke 20 to 21.9.1818, HEd 7:114, R. 1:369(107), P. 166.
11. L. 87 to John Hamilton Reynolds 22.9.1818, HEd 7:116, R. 1:370(108), P. 168.
12. L. 64 to Reynolds 3.5.1818, HEd 7:10, R. 1:282(81), P. 117.
13. L. 93 to Woodhouse 27.10.1818, HEd 7:129, R. 1:387(118), P. 172.
14. L. 90 to James Augustus Hessey 9.10.1818, HEd 7:122, R. 1:374(110), P. 170.
15. End 4:475-7, HEd 2:208, Ox 172, AEP 264-5, OSA 144.
16. L. 69 to Benjamin Bailey 10.6.1818, HEd 7:21, R. 1:293(86), P. 121—quotes the Bible, 2 Samuel 1:26.
17. End 4:513-4; 526; 527-8 HEd 2:210-11, Ox 174, AEP 266-2, OSA 145.
18. L. 123 to G. and G. Keats 14.2 to 3.5.1819, HEd 7:255, R. 2:78-9(159), P. 247-8.
19. L. 123 to G. and G. Keats 14.2 to 3.5.1819, HEd 7:256, R. 2:79(159), P. 248.
20. Ind 2:6-8, HEd 4:190, Ox 448, AEP 542, OSA 355.
21. Ind 1:5, HEd 4:189, Ox 447, AEP 542, OSA 355.
22. Ind 3:6-10, HEd 4:190, Ox 448, AEP 543, OSA 356.
23. L. 123 to G. and G. Keats 14.2 to 3.5.1819, HEd 7:255, R. 2:79(159), P. 248.
24. Ind 4:1-7, HEd 4:191, Ox 448, AEP 543, OSA 356.
25. Ind 2:10, HEd 4:190, Ox 448, AEP 543, OSA 355.
26. Ind 2:5, HEd 4:190, Ox 448, AEP 542, OSA 355.
27. William Shakespeare, *King Lear* V.ii.9-11.
28. End 4:539-40, HEd 2:211, Ox 174, AEP 267, OSA 145.
29. e.g. L. 33 to Bailey 22.11.1817 HEd 6:98 R. 1:185(43) P. 31.
30. L. 156 to G. and G. Keats 17 to 27.9.1819, HEd 8:108, R. 2:213(199), P. 355.

31. *Ibid.*
32. L. 64 to Reynolds 3.5.1818, HEd 7:9–10, R. 1:280–1(80), P. 115–6.
33. L. 32 to G. and Th. Keats 21.12.1817, HEd 6:104, R. 1:193(45), P. 53.
34. L. 64 to Reynolds 3.5.1818, HEd 7:10, R. 1:281(80), P. 116.
35. L. 123 to G. and G. Keats 14.2 to 3.5.1819, HEd 7:285, R. 2:102(159), P. 266–7.
36. L. 123 to G. and G. Keats 14.2 to 3.5.1819, HEd 7:286, R. 2:103(159), P. 267.
37. Samuel Taylor Coleridge, *Biographia Literaria* (Rest Fenner, 1817) vol. 2, p.273.
38. L. 53 to Bailey 13.3.1818, HEd 6:159, R. 1:242(67), P. 87.
39. L. 64 to Reynolds 3.5.1818, HEd 7:7, R. 1:279(80), P. 113.
40. L. 123 to G. and G. Keats 14.2 to 3.5.1819, HEd 7:259, R. 2:81(159), P. 250.
41. L. 60 to Reynolds 9.4.1818, HEd 6:186, R. 1:266(76), P. 102.
42. L. 53 to Bailey 13.3.1818, HEd 6:160, R. 1:281(80), P. 88.
43. L. 31 to Bailey 22.11.1817, HEd 6:98, R. 1:184(43), P. 48.
44. Night 3:3–8, HEd 3:147, Ox 258, AEP 526–7, OSA 207.
45. Fall of H 1:147–9, HEd 3:267, Ox 513, AEP 667, OSA 406.
46. Reynolds 89–97, HEd 4:117, Ox 487, AEP 325, OSA 383
47. L. 31 to Bailey 22.11.1817, HEd 6:98–9, R. 1:185(43), P. 49.
48. L. 31 to Bailey 22.11.1817, HEd 6:99, R. 185(43), P. 50.
49. Tomb 10–11, HEd 4:123, Ox 489, AEP 358, OSA 385.
50. John Milton, 'Paradise Lost' Book VIII, 462–3 in Rev. H.C. Beeching (ed.), *The Poetical Works of John Milton,* (London, Oxford University Press, 1914) P. 345.
51. Milton, 'Paradise Lost', Book VIII, 482–3 in Beeching (ed.) *John Milton,* P. 346.
52. L. 31 to Bailey 22.11.1817, HEd 6:98, R. 1:185(43), P. 49.
53. L. 31 to Bailey 22.11.1817, HEd 6:97–8, R. 1:184(43), P. 48.
54. L. 31 to Bailey 22.11.1817, HEd 6:98, R. 1:185(43), P. 49.
55. *Ibid.*
56. Reynolds, HEd 4:113, Ox 484, AEP 320, OSA 381.
57. L. 53 to Bailey 13.3.1818, HEd 6:162, R. 1:244(67), P. 89.
58. L. 64 to Reynolds 3.5.1818, HEd 7:11, R. 1:282(180), P. 117.
59. *Ibid.*
60. L. 64 to Reynolds 3.5.1818, HEd 7:7, R. 1:279(80), P. 113.
61. L. 64 to Reynolds 3.5.1818, HEd 7:9, R. 1:281(80), P. 115–6.
62. L. 64 to Reynolds 3.5.1818, HEd 7:11, R. 1:281(80), P. 116.
63. L. 58 to Reynolds 25.3.1818, HEd 6:182–3, R. 1:263(74), P. 99. (The painting is in the National Gallery, London.)
64. Reynolds 2–4, HEd 4:113, Ox 484, AEP 320, OSA 381.
65. Reynolds 19, HEd 4:114, Ox 485, AEP 321, OSA 381.
66. Tomb 10–11, HEd 4:123, Ox 489, AEP 358, OSA 385.

67. L. 64 to Reynolds 3.5.1818, HEd 7:11, R. 1:282(80), P. 117.
68. Reynolds 67, HEd 4:117, Ox 487, AEP 325, OSA 383.
69. L. 64 to Reynolds 3.5.1818, HEd 7:9, R. 1:281(80), P. 116.
70. Reynolds 49–51, HEd 4:115, Ox 486, AEP 323, OSA 382.
71. Reynolds 67–9, HEd 4:116, Ox 486, AEP 323, OSA 382.
72. Reynolds 71–2, HEd 4:116, Ox 486, AEP 323–4, OSA 382.
73. Reynolds 74–5, HEd 4:116, Ox 486, AEP 324, OSA 382–3.
74. Reynolds 76–7, HEd 4:116–7, Ox 486, AEP 324, OSA 383.
75. Reynolds 77, HEd 4:117, Ox 486, AEP 324, OSA 383.
76. L. 48 to Reynolds 19.2.1818, HEd 6:147, R. 1:231(62), P. 79.
77. L. 48 to Reynolds 19.2.1818, HEd 6:149, R. 1:232(62) P. 80.
78. *Ibid.*
79. Thrush 9–4, HEd 4:90, Ox 483, AEP 311, OSA 380.
80. L. 90 to Hessey 9.10.1818, HEd 7:122, R. 1:374(110), P. 170.
81. L. 31 to Bailey 22.11.1817, HEd 6:98, R. 1:184(43), P. 48.
82. L. 60 to Reynolds, HEd 6:186, R. 1:266(76), P. 102.
83. L. 94 to G. and Th. Keats 14 to 31.10.1818, HEd 7:147–8, R. 1:403(120), P. 187.

Chapter 4

1. L. 64 to Reynolds 3.5.1818, HEd 7:9, R. 1:218(80), P. 116.
2. Grec 1:3–4, HEd 3:153, Ox 260, AEP 533, OSA 209.
3. Night 1:10, HEd 3:146, Ox 257, AEP 525, OSA 207.
4. Night 2:9, HEd 3:146, Ox 257, AEP 526, OSA 207.
5. Night 2:1, 9:10, HEd 3:146, Ox 257, AEP 525–6, OSA 207.
6. Night 8:10, HEd 3:151, Ox 260, AEP 532, OSA 209.
7. Night 4:5, HEd 3:148, Ox 258, AEP 527, OSA 208.
8. Night 2:1, HEd 3:146, Ox 257, AEP 525, OSA 207.
9. Night 4:1–3, HEd 3:147–8, Ox 258, AEP 527, OSA 208.
10. Night 3:4, HEd 3:147, Ox 258, AEP 526, OSA 207.
11. Night 5:1–2, HEd 3:148, Ox 258, AEP 528, OSA 208.
12. Night 5:3, HEd 3:148, Ox 258, AEP 528, OSA 208.
13. Night 5:3–10, HEd 3:148–9, Ox 258–9, AEP 528, OSA 208.
14. Night 6:5–6, HEd 3:149, Ox 259, AEP 529, OSA 208.
15. Night 3:5–6, HEd 3:147, Ox 258, AEP 526–7, OSA 207.
16. Night 6:1–5, HEd 3:149, Ox 259, AEP 529, OSA 208.
17. Night 6:1–10, HEd 3:149, Ox 260, AEP 529, OSA 207.
18. Night 8:6–7, HEd 3:151, Ox 257, AEP 532, OSA 209.
19. Night 1:10, HEd 3:145, Ox 257, AEP 525, OSA 207.

20. *See* the account of Charles Brown in H.E. Rollins (ed.), *The Keats Circle: Letters and Papers 1816–1879*, (Cambridge, Mass., Harvard University Press, 1942) vol. 2, p. 65.
21. Night 1:8–9, HEd 3:145, Ox 260, AEP 525, OSA 207.
22. Grec 2:1, HEd 3:154, Ox 261, AEP 534, OSA 209.
23. Grec 2:1–2, HEd 3:154, Ox 261, AEP 534–5, OSA 209.
24. Grec 1:1; 1:1; 1:2, HEd 3:153, Ox 260, AEP 533, OSA 209. *See also:* ch. 3, p.43ff.
25. Grec 2:2–4, HEd 3:154, Ox 261, AEP 535, OSA 209.
26. Grec 1:5–6, HEd 3:153, Ox 260, AEP 534, OSA 209.
27. Grec 1:3–4, HEd 3:153, Ox 260, AEP 533, OSA 209.
28. It is surely no accident that the nightingale is a bird and the figures on the urn are human.
29. Night 2:9 to 3:2, HEd 3:154, Ox 257–8, AEP 535, OSA 207.
30. *See* Martin Heidegger, 'Vorträge und Aufsätze', vol. II, p.66 in A Hofstadter (trans.) *Poetry, Language, Thought* (London, Harper and Row, 1971) p.217–8.
31. Grec 3:5–7; 2:9–10, HEd 3:154, Ox 261, AEP 535, OSA 210.
32. Grec 3:6–7; 3:4; 2:10, HEd 3:154–5, Ox 261, AEP 535, OSA 210.
33. Grec 2:8–9; 2:5–6; 3:1–2, HEd 3:154, Ox 261, AEP 535, OSA 210.
34. Grec 2:10; 3:6–7, HEd 3:154–5, Ox 261, AEP 535, OSA 210.
35. Grec 5:1–3, HEd 3:156, Ox 262, AEP 537, OSA 210.
36. Grec 3:9–10, HEd 3:155, Ox 261, AEP 536, OSA 210.
37. Grec 5:4–5, HEd 3:156, Ox 262, AEP 537, OSA 210.
38. Reynolds 67–71, HEd 4:116, Ox 486, AEP 323, OSA 382.
39. Reynolds 71–2, HEd 4:116, Ox 486, AEP 323–4, OSA 382.
40. Reynolds 93–7; 102–5, HEd 4:117–8, Ox 487, AEP 325, OSA 382.
41. L. 123 to G. and G. Keats 14.2 to 3.5.1819, HEd 7:256, R. 2:79(159), P. 248.
42. Reynolds 74–5; 76, HEd 4:116–7, Ox 486, AEP 324, OSA 382–3.
43, L. 31 to Bailey 22.11.1817, HEd 6:98, R. 1:185(43), P. 49.
44. L. 64 to Reynolds 3.5.1818, HEd 7:9, R. 1:281(80), P. 115.
45. L. 64 to Reynolds 3.5.1818, HEd 7:9, R. 1:280–1(80), P. 115.
46. L. 64 to Reynolds 3.5.1818, HEd 7:9, R. 1:281(80), P. 115–6.
47. Reynolds 102, HEd 4:118, Ox 487, AEP 325, OSA 382.
48. L. 64 to Reynolds 3.5.1818, HEd 7:9–10, R. 1:281(80), P. 115–6.
49. Reynolds 78–82, HEd 4:117, Ox 486, AEP 324, OSA 382.
50. L. 60 to Reynolds 9.4.1818, HEd 6:186, R. 1:266(76), P. 102.
51. L. 186 to Fanny Brawne ?.2.1820, HEd 8:169, R. 2:263(231), P. 392.
52. *See*: John Middleton Murry, *Keats and Shakespeare* (London, Oxford University Press, 1958) p. 73.
53. L. 94 to G. and G. Keats 14 to 31.10.1818, HEd 7:148, R. 1:403(120), P. 187.
54. L. 98 to G. and G. Keats 16.12.1818 to 4.1.1819, HEd 7:176, R.

2:19(137), P. 207.
55.   L. 32 to G. and Th. Keats 21.12.1817, HEd 6:103, R. 1:192(45), P. 52.
56.   L. 32 to G. and Th. Keats 21.12.1817, HEd 6:104, R. 1:194(45), P. 52.
57.   Grec 5:8, HEd 3:157, Ox 261, AEP 537, OSA 210.
58.   L. 32 to G. and G. Keats 21.12.1817, HEd 6:104, R. 1:193(45), P. 5.
59.   *Ibid.*
60.   L. 93 to Woodhouse 27.10.1818, HEd 7:129, R. 1:386–7(118), P. 172.
61.   L. 93 to Woodhouse 27.10.1818, HEd 7:130, R. 1:387(118), P. 172.
62.   *Ibid.*
63.   L. 90 to Hessey 9.10.1818, HEd 7:122, R. 1:374(110), P. 170.
64.   L. 123 to G. and G. Keats 14.2 to 3.5.1819, HEd 7:255, R. 2:78–9(159),
      P. 247.
65.   L. 48 to Reynolds 19.2.1818, HEd 6:149, R. 1:232(62), P. 80.
66.   L. 123 to G. and G. Keats 14.2 to 3.5.1819, HEd 7:256, R. 2:79(159). P.
      248.
67.   L. 123 to G. and G. Keats 14.2 to 3.5.1819, HEd 7:255, R. 2:79(159), P.
      248.
68.   *Ibid.*
69.   L. 93 to Woodhouse 27.10.1818, HEd 7:130, R. 1:387(118), P. 172.
70.   L. 48 to Reynolds 19.2.1818, HEd 6:147, R. 1:231(62), P. 79.
71.   Ind 1:5, HEd 4:189, Ox 447, AEP 542, OSA 355.
72.   Ind 2:1–5, HEd 4:190, Ox 447–8, AEP 542, OSA 355.
73.   Ind 2:5, HEd 4:190, Ox 448, AEP 542, OSA 355.
74.   Ind 2:6–7, HEd 4:190, Ox 448, AEP 542, OSA 355.
75.   Ind 4:3; 5:1 HEd 4:190–1(3:3;4:1), Ox 448, AEP 543(3:3;4:1), OSA 356.
76.   Ind 4:3–4, HEd 4:190(3:3–4), Ox 449, AEP 543(3:3–4), OSA 356.
77.   L. 32 to G. and Th. Keats 21.12.1817, HEd 6:104, R. 1:193(45), P. 32.
78.   *Ibid.*
79.   Ind 5:1, HEd 4:191(4:1), Ox 448, AEP 543(4:1), OSA 356.
80.   Ind 4:4, HEd 4:190(3:4), Ox 448, AEP 543(3:4), OSA 356.
81.   Ind 5:2–7, HEd 4:191(4:2–7), Ox 448, AEP 543(4:2–7), OSA 356.
82.   Ind 6:5–6, HEd 4:192, Ox 449, AEP 544, OSA 357.
83.   Grec 5:4–5, HEd 3:156, Ox 262, AEP 537, OSA 210.
84.   L. 31 to Bailey 22.11.1817, HEd 6:98, R. 1:185(43), P. 49.
85.   L. 31 to Bailey 22.11.1817, HEd 6:97, R. 1:184(43), P. 48.
86.   L. 31 to Bailey 22.11.1817, HEd 6:97–8, R. 1:184(43), P. 48.
87.   L. 31 to Bailey 22.11.1817, HEd 6:97, R. 1:184(43), P. 48.
88.   L. 31 to Bailey 22.11.1817, HEd 6:97–8, R. 1:184(43), P. 48.
89.   Melan 3:2, HEd 3:1, Ox 275, AEP 540, OSA 220.
90.   Night 3:9–10, HEd 3:147, Ox 258, AEP 527, OSA 207.
91.   Grec 1:6, HEd 3:153, Ox 260, AEP 534, OSA 209.
92.   Grec 5:9–10, HEd 3:157, Ox 266, AEP 537, OSA 210.

Chapter 5

1. L. 56 to G. and G. Keats 17 to 27.9.1819, HEd 8:107, R. 2:212(19), P. 354.
2. Blake, 'Marriage of Heaven and Hell' Plates 5–6, AEP 106–7, OSA 149–50.
3. Blake, 'There is no Natural Religion', 2nd series:7, OSA 97–8.
4. Blake, 'Marriage of Heaven and Hell', Plate 4, AEP 106, OSA 149.
5. Blake, 'The French Revolution' 189, AEP 137, OSA 142.
6. Blake, 'Marriage of Heaven and Hell' Plate 11, AEP 111, OSA 153.
7. *Ibid.*
8. *Ibid.*
9. *Ibid.*
10. Blake, 'To Nobodaddy', AEP 155, OSA 171 and 'Let the Brothels of Paris be opened' 9f, AEP 168, OSA 185.
11. Blake, 'Marriage of Heaven and Hell' Plate 6, AEP 107, OSA 150.
12. Blake. 'Jerusalem' Plate 77, AEP 794, OSA 716–7.
13. Blake, 'Milton' Plate 4, 1:29, OSA 484.
14. Martin Heidegger, 'Vorträge und Aufsätze' vol. II, p.67 in A. Hofstadter (trans.) *Poetry, Language, Thought* (London, Harper and Row, 1971) p.218–9.
15. Blake, 'Marriage of Heaven and Hell' Plate 3, AEP 105, OSA 149.
16. Blake, 'Milton' Plate 28:62 to Plate 29:3, AEP 538, OSA 516.
17. L. 31 to Benjamin Bailey 22.11.1817, HEd 6:98, R. 1:185(43), P. 49.
18. Blake, 'Milton' Plate 35:42, AEP 550, OSA 526.
19. Blake, 'Milton' Plate 41:37, AEP 564, OSA 534.
20. Blake, 'Milton' Plate 42:2, AEP 564, OSA 534.
21. Blake, 'Vala or the Four Zoas' Night VIIa:344–5, AEP 384(340–1), OSA 328.
22. Blake, 'Milton' Plate 32:32, AEP 574, OSA 522.
23. Blake, 'Marriage of Heaven and Hell' Plate 16, AEP 115, OSA 155.
24. Blake, 'Marriage of Heaven and Hell' Plates 5 and 6, AEP 107, OSA 150.
25. *See* John Middleton Murry, *William Blake* (New York, McGraw-Hill, 1964) p. 214–6.
26. Blake, 'Milton' Plate 14:28–9, AEP 505–6, OSA 495–6.
27. Blake, 'Milton' Plate 14:22–4, AEP 505, OSA 495.
28. Blake, 'Vala or the Four Zoas', Night VIIa:344–5, AEP 384(340–1), OSA 328.
29. Blake, 'Milton' Plate 28:62 to Plate 29:3, AEP 538, OSA 516.
30. Blake, 'Milton' Plate 40:35, AEP 563, OSA 533.
31. Blake, 'Milton' Plate 42:5–6, AEP 564, OSA 534.
32. Blake, 'Milton' Plate 41:1–2, AEP 563, OSA 533.
33. L. 31 to Bailey 22.11.1817, HEd 6:97, R. 1:184(43), P. 48.
34. Blake, 'Milton' Plate 13:50; 13:51 to 14:2, AEP 504, OSA 495.
35. The underlying theme of this section is present in John Middleton

Murry, 'The Final Struggle', ch. 10 of his *Keats and Shakespeare* (London, Oxford University Press, 1958) p. 149 ff.
36. L. 41 to G. and Th. Keats 23.1.1818, HEd 6:127, R. 1:214(56), P. 67.
37. L. 32 to G. and Th. Keats 21.12.1817, HEd 6:104, R. 1:193(45), P.53.
38. *Ibid.*
39. William Hazlitt, 'Lectures on the English Poets' in P.P. Howe (ed.), *The Complete Works*, (London, Dent, 1930) vol. 5, p. 47.
40. Hazlitt, 'English Poets' in Howe (ed.), *The Complete Works*, vol. 5, p. 48.
41. Hazlitt, 'English Poets' in Howe (ed.), *The Complete Works*, vol. 5, p. 50.
42. *Ibid.*
43. Hazlitt, 'English Poets' in Howe (ed.), *The Complete Works*, vol. 5, p. 51.
44. *Ibid.*
45. Hazlitt, 'English Poets' in Howe (ed.), *The Complete Works*, vol. 5, p. 52.
46. Hazlitt, 'English Poets' in Howe (ed.), *The Complete Works*, vol. 5, p. 52.
47. Hazlitt, 'English Poets' in Howe (ed.), *The Complete Works*, vol. 5, p. 58.
48. *Ibid.*
49. Milton HEd 4:72, Ox 479, AEP 292, OSA 377. *Also*: L. 40 to Bailey 23.1.1818, HEd 6:123, R. 1:211(55), P. 64.
50. Lear, HEd 4:67, Ox 483, AEP 295, OSA 380. *Also*: L. 41 to G. and Th. Keats 23.1.1818, HEd 6:128, R. 1:214–5(56), P. 68.
51. Milton 1–5, HEd 4:72, Ox 479, AEP 293, OSA 377.
52. Hazlitt, 'English Poets' in Howe (ed.), *The Complete Works*, vol. 5, p. 56.
53. Milton 6–10; 23–8, HEd 4:72;74, Ox 479;480, AEP 293;293–4, OSA 377;378.
54. Lear 1–8, HEd 2:76–7, Ox 483, AEP 295–6, OSA 380.
55. Lear 12–14, HEd 4:77, Ox 493, AEP 296, OSA 380.
56. L. 93 to Woodhouse 27.10.1818, HEd 7:129, R. 1:387, P. 172.
57. L. 31 to Bailey 22.11.1817, HEd 6:97–8, R. 1:185(43), P. 49.
58. L. 31 to Bailey 22.11.1817, HEd 6:98, R. 1:185(43), P. 49.
59. L. 60 to Reynolds 9.4.1818, HEd 6:186, R. 1:266(76), P. 182.
60. Tomb 10, HEd 4:123, Ox 489, AEP 358, OSA 385.
61. L. 127 to Miss Jeffrey 31.5.1819, HEd 7:298, R. 2:113(164), P. 273.
62. L. 133 to Haydon 17.6.1819, HEd 7:307, R. 2:120(170), P.279.
63. *Ibid.*
64. *Ibid.*
65. L. 133 to Haydon 17.6.1819, HEd 7:308, R. 2:120(170), P. 280.
66. L. 132 to Fanny Keats 17.6.1819, HEd 7:306, R. 2:122(171), P. 279.

67. L. 132 to Fanny Keats 17.6.1819, HEd 7:305, R. 2:121(171), P. 278.
68. L. 127 to Miss Jeffrey 31.5.1819, HEd 7:297, R. 2:113(164), P. 273.
69. L. 127 to Miss Jeffrey 31.5.1819, HEd 7:297, R. 2:112–3(164), P. 273.
70. L. 127 to Miss Jeffrey 31.5.1819, HEd 7:297, R. 2:113(164), P. 273.
71. L. 127 to Miss Jeffrey 31.5.1819, HEd 7:297, R. 2:112(164), P. 273.
72. *Ibid.*
73. L. 132 to Fanny Keats 17.6.1819, HEd 7:305, R. 2:121(171), P. 278.
74. L. 51 to John Taylor 27.2.1818, HEd 6:155, R. 1:238–9(65), P. 84.
75. Ind 6:1–4, HEd 4:191–2, Ox 449, AEP 544, OSA 356.
76. Ind 6:5–6, HEd 4:192, Ox 449, AEP 544, OSA 357.
77. L. 127 to Miss Jeffrey 31.5.1819, HEd 7:298, R. 2:113(164), P. 273.
78. L. 127 to Miss Jeffrey 31.5.1819, HEd 7:297, R. 2:113(164), P. 273.
79. L. 115 to Haydon 8.3.1819, HEd 7:213, R. 2:43(149), P. 220.
80. L. 136 to Fanny Brawne 8.7.1819, HEd 8:10, R. 2:127(174), P. 286.
81. L. 137 to Reynolds 11.7.1819, HEd 8:11, R. 2:128(175), P. 287.
82. *Ibid.*
83. L. 129 to Fanny Keats 9.6.1819, HEd 7:302, R. 2:117(167), P. 277,
84. L. 137 to Reynolds 11.7.1819, HEd 8:10–11, R. 2:128(175), P. 286–7.
85. L. 142 to Bailey 14.8.1819, HEd 8:25, R. 2:139(181), P. 297.
86. L. 134 to Brawne 1.7.1819, HEd 8:4–5, R. 2:123(172), P. 281.
87. L. 138 to Brawne 15.7.1819, HEd 8:15, R. 2:131(176), P. 289–90.
88. L. 139 to Brawne 25.7.1819, HEd 8:16–17, R. 2:132–3(178), P. 290–1.
89. L. 141 to Brawne 5 to 6.8.1819, HEd 8:23, R. 2:137(180), P. 295–6.
90. L. 143 to Brawne 16.8.1819, HEd 8:27–8, R. 2:140–1(182), P. 298–90.
91. L. 143 to Brawne 16.8.1819, HEd 8:29–30, R. 2:142(182), P. 301.
92. L. 143 to Brawne 16.8.1819, HEd 8:28, R. 2:141(182), P. 300.
93. L. 150 to Brawne 13.9.1819, HEd 8:46–7, R. 2:160(191), P. 313.
94. Hazlitt, 'English Poets' in Howe (ed.), *The Complete Works*, vol. 5, p. 57.
95. L. 142 to Bailey 14.8.1819, HEd 8:25–6, R. 2:139(181), P. 297–8.
96. L. 145 to Reynolds 24.8.1819, HEd 8:33–4, R. 2:146(185), P. 304.
97. L. 144 to Taylor 23.8.1819, HEd 8:31, R. 2:144(183), P. 302.
98. L. 145 to Reynolds 24.8.1819, HEd 8:34, R. 2:146(185), P. 304.
99. John Milton, 'Paradise Lost' in Rev. H.C. Beeching (ed.), *The Poetical Works of John Milton*, (London, Oxford University Press, 1914) Book I, 571–2, p. 195.
100. L. 145 to Reynolds 24.8.1819, HEd 8:34, R. 2:146(185), P. 304.
101. L. 144 to Taylor 23.8.1819, HEd 8:31, R. 2:144(183), P. 302.
102. L. 32 to G. and T. Keats 21.12.1917, HEd 6:104, R. 1:193(45), P. 53.
103. L. 145 to Reynolds 24.8.1819, HEd 8:34, R. 2:146(185), P. 304.
104. L. 93 to Woodhouse 27.10.1818, HEd 7:130, R. 1:387(118), P. 172.
105. L. 93 to Woodhouse 27.10.1818, HEd 7:129, R. 1:387(118), P. 172.
106. Ind 6:1, HEd 4:191, Ox 449, AEP 544, OSA 356.
107. Ind 2:1, HEd 4:190, Ox 448, AEP 542, OSA 355.

108. Ind 6:6, HEd 4:192, Ox 449, AEP 544, OSA 357.
109. Ind 6:3, HEd 4:192, Ox 449, AEP 544, OSA 356.
110. L. 150 to Brawne 13.9.1819, HEd 8:46, R. 2:160(191), P. 313.
111. L. 150 to Brawne 13.9.1819, HEd 8:47, R. 2:160(191), P. 313-4.
112. L. 151 to Reynolds 21.9.1819, HEd 8:49, R. 2:167(193), P. 31.
113. L. 156 to G. and G. Keats 17 to 27.9.1819, HEd 8:106, R. 2:212(199), P. 353.
114. L. 156 to G. and G. Keats 17 to 27.9.1819, HEd 8:107, R. 2:212(199), P. 354.
115. *Ibid.*
116. L. 156 to G. and G. Keats 17 to 27.9.1819, HEd 8:106-7, R. 2:212(199), P. 353-4.
117. L. 151 to Reynolds 21.9.1819, HEd 8:49, R. 2:167(193), P. 31.
118. Lord Houghton (ed.), *The Life and Letters of John Keats* (London, Edward Moxon, 1867) p. 103. *See also*: HEd 2:18 and note AEP 120.
119. Mathew 55-8, HEd 1:55, Ox 29, AEP 26, OSA 24.
120 L. 64 to Reynolds 3.5.1818, HEd 7:9, R. 1:281(80), P. 115-6.
121. L. 142 to Bailey 14.8.1819, HEd 8:25, R. 2:139(181), P. 297-8.
122. William Sharp, *Life and Letters of Joseph Severn* (London, Sampson Low, Marston and Co., 1892) p. 182.

Chapter 6

1. L. 64 to Reynolds 3.5.1818, HEd 7:9-10, R. 1:280-1(80), P. 115-6.
2. L. 64 to Reynolds 3.5.1818, HEd 7:10, R. 1:281(80), P. 116.
3. *Ibid.*
4. Fall of H 1:150, HEd 3:267, Ox 513, AEP 667, OSA 406.
5. L. 31 to Bailey 22.11.1817, HEd 6:98, R. 1:185(43), P. 49.
6. L. 151 to Reynolds 21.9.1819, HEd 8:39, R. 2:167(193), P. 315.
7. *Ibid.*
8. William Hazlitt, 'Lectures on the English Poets' in P.P. Howe (ed.), *The Complete Works*, (London, Dent, 1930) vol. 5, p. 50.
9. Fall of H 1:142-3, HEd 3:266, Ox 513, AEP 666, OSA 406.
10. Fall of H 1:148-9, HEd 3:267, Ox 513, AEP 667, OSA 406.
11. Fall of H 1:226-7, HEd 3:270, Ox 515, AEP 672, OSA 408.
12. Fall of H 1:290, HEd 3:272, Ox 517, AEP 675, OSA 410.
13. Fall of H 1:357-8, HEd 3:275, Ox 518, AEP 678, OSA 411-2.
14. Fall of H 1:227, HEd 3:270, Ox 515, AEP 672, OSA 408.
15. Fall of H 1:228-30, HEd 3:270, Ox 515, AEP 672, OSA 408.
16. Fall of H 1:154; 156-9, HEd 3:267, Ox 513, AEP 667-8, OSA 406-7.

17. Fall of H 1:165, HEd 3:268, Ox 513, AEP 668, OSA 407.
18. Fall of H 163–4, HEd 3:268, Ox 513, AEP 668, OSA 407.
19. Fall of H 1:1–2, HEd 3:261, Ox 509, AEP 657, OSA 403.
20. Fall of H 1:2–4, HEd 3:261, Ox 509, AEP 657, OSA 403.
21. Fall of H 1:4–6, HEd 3:261, Ox 509, AEP 657, OSA 403.
22. Fall of H 1:7, HEd 3:261, Ox 509, AEP 657, OSA 403.
23. Fall of H 1:156–9, HEd 3:267, Ox 513, AEP 668, OSA 407.
24. Fall of H 1:7, HEd 3:261, Ox 509, AEP 657, OSA 403.
25. Fall of H 1:8, HEd 3:261, Ox 509, AEP 658, OSA 403.
26. Fall of H 1:9, HEd 3:261, Ox 509, AEP 658, OSA 403.
27. Fall of H 1:11, HEd 3:261, Ox 509, AEP 658, OSA 403.
28. Fall of H 1:9–11, HEd 3:261, Ox 509, AEP 658, OSA 403.
29. Why did 12, HEd 4:194, Ox 470, AEP 488, OSA 370.
30. Ind 3:6–10, HEd 4:190, Ox 448, AEP 543, OSA 356.
31. Why did 13–14, HEd 4:194, Ox 470, AEP 488, OSA 370.
32. See Martin Heidegger, 'Holswege' (Klosterman, Frankfurt, 1972) P.279 in A. Hofstadter (trans.), *Poetry, Language, Thought* (London, Harper and Row, 1971) p. 214.
33. Fall of H 1:141–4, HEd 3:266–7, Ox 512–3, AEP 666, OSA 406.
34. L. 64 to Reynolds 3.5.1818, HEd 7:9, R. 1:281(80), P. 115–6.
35. L. 64 to Reynolds 3.5.1818, HEd 7:10, R. 1:281(80), P. 116.
36. *Ibid.*
37. Fall of H 1:175–6, HEd 3:268, Ox 513–4, AEP 669, OSA 407.
38. Fall of H 1:169, HEd 3:268, Ox 513, AEP 668, OSA 407.
39. Fall of H 1:147–9, HEd 3:267, Ox 513, AEP 667, OSA 406.
40. L. 93 to Woodhouse 27.10.1818, HEd 7:129–30, R. 1:386–7(118), P. 172.
41. Fall of H 1:165, HEd 3:268, Ox 513, AEP 668, OSA 407.
42. Fall of H 1:162, HEd 3:268, Ox 513, AEP 668, OSA 407.
43. Fall of H 1:184, HEd 3:268, Ox 514, AEP 669, OSA 407.
44. Fall of H 1:182, HEd 3:268, Ox 514, AEP 669, OSA 407.
45. Fall of H 1:166, HEd 3:268, Ox 513, AEP 668, OSA 407.
46. Hazlitt, 'English Poets' in Howe (ed.) *The Complete Works*, vol. 5, p. 47.
47. Fall of H 1:169–74 HEd 3:268, Ox 513, AEP 668–9, OSA 407.
48. Hazlitt 'English Poets' in Howe (ed.), *The Complete Works*, vol. 5, p. 51.
49. Lamia 1:192–6, HEd 3:21–2, Ox 196, AEP 625, OSA 165–6.
50. Reynolds 74–7, HEd 4:116–7, Ox 486, AEP 324, OSA 382–3.
51. Fall of H 1:160, HEd 3:267, Ox 513, AEP 668, OSA 407.
52. L. 123 to G. and G. Keats 14.2 to 3.5.1819, HEd 7:258–9, R. 2:80–1(159); P. 250 quotes Milton, 'A Maske Presented at Ludlow Castle' (Comus) lines 476–8, in Beeching (ed.) *John Milton*, p.61.
53. John Milton, 'Paradise Lost', Book III:135–7, in H.C. Beeching (ed.) *The Poetical Works of John Milton* (London, Oxford University Press, 1914) p. 231.
54. Marginalia to John Milton, 'Paradise Lost', Book III:135–7, HEd

5:301.
55. Blake, 'Marriage of Heaven and Hell' Plate 4:3, AEP 106, OSA 149.
56. L. 123 to G. and G. Keats 14.2 to 3.5.1819, HEd 7:258, R. 2:80(159), P. 250.
57. L. 142 to Bailey 14.8.1819, HEd 8:24, R. 2:139(181), P. 298.
58. L. 31 to Bailey 22.11.1817, HEd 6:98, R. 1:185(43), P. 49.
59. L. 123 to G. and G. Keats, 14.2 to 3.5.1819, HEd 7:258, R. 2:80(159), P. 250.
60. *Ibid.*
61. Hyp 3:84-6, HEd 3:249, Ox 303, AEP 438, OSA 241.
62. *See* the parallel development between the 'Ode to a Nightingale' and the 'Ode on a Grecian Urn' in ch. 4, p.62ff.
63. Hyp 3:87, HEd 3:249, Ox 303, AEP 438, OSA 241.
64. Hyp 3:91, HEd 3:249, Ox 303, AEP 438, OSA 241.
65. Hyp 3:59-67, HEd 3:248, Ox 302, AEP 437-8, OSA 241.
66. Fall of H 3:302-4, HEd 3:273, Ox 517, AEP 676, OSA 410.
67. Hyp 3:99-102, HEd 3:250, Ox 303, AEP 439, OSA 242.
68. Hyp 3:113, HEd 3:250, Ox 304, AEP 440, OSA 242.
69. Hyp 3:111-3, HEd 3:250, Ox 304, AEP 439-40, OSA 242.
70. Hyp 3:129, HEd 3:252, Ox 304, AEP 441, OSA 242.
71. Hyp 3:114-9, HEd 3:250, Ox 304, AEP 440, OSA 242.
72. Hyp 3:124-30, HEd 3:251-2, Ox 304, AEP 440-1, OSA 242.
73. Hyp 3:112, HEd 3:250, Ox 304, AEP 439, OSA 242.
74. Fall of H 1:141-4, HEd 3:266-7, Ox 512-3, AEP 666, OSA 406.
75. L. 156 to G. and G. Keats 17 to 27.9.1819, HEd 8:106, R. 2:212(199), P. 353.
76. Fall of H 1:175, HEd 3:268, Ox 513, AEP 669, OSA 407.
77. Fall of H 1:168-9, HEd 3:268, Ox 513, AEP 668, OSA 407.
78. Fall of H 1:162, HEd 3:268, Ox 513, AEP 668, OSA 407.
79. Fall of H 1:166, HEd 3:268, Ox 513, AEP 668, OSA 407.
80. Fall of H 1:388-90, HEd 3:276, Ox 519, AEP 680, OSA 412.
81. Fall of H 1:143-4, HEd 3:266-7, Ox 513, AEP 666, OSA 406.
82. Fall of H 1:251-71, HEd 3:271, Ox 516, AEP 673-5, OSA 409.
83. Fall of H 1:397-8, HEd 3:276, Ox 519, AEP 680, OSA 412-3.
84. Hyp 3:129, HEd 3:252, Ox 304, AEP 441, OSA 242.
85. Grec 1:6, HEd 3:153, Ox 260, AEP 533. OSA 209.
86. Grec 5:4, HEd 3:156, Ox 262, AEP 537, OSA 210.
87. Fall of H 1:390, HEd 3:276, Ox 519, AEP 680, OSA 412.
88. Fall of H 1:400-1, HEd 3:276, Ox 519, AEP 680, OSA 413.
89. Fall of H—Title, HEd 3:255, Ox 509, AEP 655, OSA 403.
90. Grec 5:9-10, HEd 3:157, Ox 262, AEP 537, OSA 210.

Postface

1. Hannah Arendt, 'Willing', *The Life of the Mind* (London, Secker and Warburg, 1978) vol. 2, p. 119.

2. 'It hides itself in making the object visible'. *See* Merleau-Ponty, 'Eye and Mind', 'L'Oeil et L'esprit', (Paris, Gallimard, 1964) p.29–30. Carlton Dalley (trans.) in J.M. Edie (ed.), *The Primacy of Perception*, (Evanston, Northwestern University Press, 1964) P. 167.

3. Martin Heidegger, *Vorträge und Aufsätze*, (Neske, 1967) vol. I, p. 14–15; in W. Lovitt (trans.), *The Question Concerning Technology* (London, Harper and Row, 1971) p. 14–15.

4. So the critic 'must first turn, turn back to where we are in reality already standing ... [and] not prematurely break off the dialogue we have begun with the poetic experience'. *See* Heidegger, *Unterwegs Zur Sprache* (Tübingen Neske, 1971), p. 190–1; in P.D. Hertz (trans) *On the Way to Language* (London, Harper and Row, 1971), P. 85.

5. *See* Hans-Georg Gadamer, *Warheit und Method*, (Tubingen, J.C.B. Mohr, 1960) p. 182; in G. Bardon and J. Cumming (trans. and eds.) *Truth and Method*, (London, Sheed and Ward, 1975) P. 325 ff. *Also*: Jose Ortega Y. Gasset, 'Unas Lecciones de Metafisica', in *Obras Completas* (Madrid, Revista de Occidente, 1966) vol. 4, p.219 in Mildred Adams (trans) *Some Lessons in Metaphysics*, (New York,W.W. Norton, 1969) p.15–16.

6. John Keats L. 32 to G. and Th. Keats 21.12.1817, HEd 6:104, R 1:193(45) P.53.

7. *See* Heidegger, *Sein und Zeit* (Tübingen, Niemeyer, 1972) p. 156–7; in J. Macquarrie and E. Robinson (trans.), *Being and Time*, (Oxford, Basil Blackwell, 1967) p. 199.

8. Heidegger, *Sein und Zeit*, pp. 157–8; Macquarrie and Robinson (trans.) *Being in Time*, p. 200.

9. Heidegger, 'Das Wesen der Sprache', in *Unterwegs zur Sprache*, (Neske, 1971) p. 186; P.D. Hertz (trans.) 'The Nature of Language' in *On the Way to Language*, p. 81.

10. 'Cuius genera sunt tria: unum vernaculum ac domi natum, alterum adventicium tertium notham ex peregrino hic natum', Varo, *On the Latin Language*, with a trans. by R.C. Kent, 'Loeb Classical Texts', (Cambridge, Mass., Harvard University Press, 1938) Book X:69; vol. 2, p. 585.

11. 'Multi utantur non modo poetae, sed etiam plerique omnes qui soluta oratione loquuntur', Ibid.

12. Antonio de Nebrija the Elder, *Grammatica Castellana* (Salamanca, 1492).

13. Heidegger, *Unterwegs zur Sprache* (Tübingen, Neske, 1971) p. 161–2; P.D. Hertz (trans.) *On the Way to Language*, p. 59.

14. Nadezhda Mandelstam, *Hope against Hope*; Max Hayward (trans.),

(London, Penguin Books, 1975), P. 85.

15. Heidegger, *Erläuterungen zu Hölderlins Dichtung* (Frankfurt, Klosterman, 1971) p. 84.

17. A good summary of these points is contained in Robert Bernasconi, 'The Experience of Language' in David Wood (ed.) *Heidegger and Language* (Warwick, Parousia Press, University of Warwick, 1981) p. 4 ff.

18. Heidegger, *Sein und Zeit* ff. (Tübingen, Niemeyer, 1972) section 16, p. 72 ff:, in MacQuarrie and Robinson (trans. and eds.) *Being and Time*, p. 102 ff.

Select Bibliography

KEATS

Texts

Arlott, Miriam (ed.), *The Poems of John Keats*, London, Longman 1957.

Forman, H. Buxton (ed.), *The Poetical Works and Other Writings of John Keats*, New York, Phaeton Press, 1970.

Garrod, H.W. (ed.), *John Keats: Poetical Works*, London, Oxford University Press. 1956.
The Poetical Works of John Keats, London, Oxford University Press, 1956.

Page, F. (ed.), *Letters of John Keats*, World Classics, London, Oxford University Press, 1956.

Rollins, H.E. (ed.), *The Letters of John Keats*, Cambridge, Cambridge University Press, 1958.

Biographies

Gittings, Robert, *John Keats*, Harmondsworth, Penguin Books, 1971.

Hewlitt, Dorothy, *A Life of John Keats*, London, Hutchinson, 1970.

Houghton, Lord — Richard Monckton Milnes — *The Life of John Keats*, London, Dent, Everymans Library, 1927.

Lowell, Amy, *John Keats*, London, Cape, 1925, 2 vols.

Richardson, Joanna, *Fanny Brawne: A Biography*, London, Thames and Hudson, 1963.

Rollins, H.E., *The Keats Circle*, Cambridge, Mass., Harvard University Press, 1948, 2 vols.

Ward, Aileen, *John Keats. The Making of a Poet*, New York, The Viking Press, 1963.

BLAKE

Texts

Keynes, Geoffrey (ed.), *Blake: Complete Writings*, Oxford, Oxford

University Press, 1966.
The Letters of William Blake, Oxford, The Clarendon Press, 1980.
Stevenson, W.H. (ed.), *the Poems of William Blake*, London, Longman, 1971.

Philosophy Texts

Biemal, Walter, *Heidegger*, Rowohlts Monographien, 1973, trans. J.L. Mehta. *Martin Heidegger: An Illustrated Study*, New York, Harcourt Brace Jovanovitch, 1976.

Gadamer, Hans-Georg, *Warheit und Methode*, Tübingen, J.C.B. Mohr, 1960, trans. as *Truth and Method*, London, Sheed and Ward, 1976.

Heidegger, Martin, 'Der Ursprung des Kunstwerkes' and 'Wozu Dichter' in *Hohlzwege*, Frankfurt, Klostermann, 1972 ('Dichterisch wohnet der Mensch', *Vorträge und Aufsätze*, Neske, 1967, all in trans. Albert Hofstadter, *Poetry, Language, Thought*, New York, Harper and Row, 1971.

Unterwegs zur Sprache, Neske, 1971, trans. P.D. Hertz, *On the Way to Language*, London, Harper and Row, 1971.

'Erläuterungen zu Hölderlins Dichtung', Frankfurt, Klostermann, 1971 of which 'Remembrance of the Past' and 'Hölderlin and the Essence of Poetry' are in trans. Douglas Scott, *Existence and Being*, London.Vision Press, 1949.

Merleau-Ponty, Maurice, *La Prose du Monde*, Paris, Gallimard, 1969, trans. John O'Neill, *the Prose of the World*, London, Heinemann, 1974.

'Le Langage Indirect et les Voix de Silence' and 'Sur la Phénoménologie du Langage', in *Signes*, Paris, Gallimard, 1960, both in trans. Richard C. McCleary, *Signs*, Evanston, Northwestern University Press, 1964.

Le Visible et l'Invisible, Paris, Gallimard, 1964, trans. Alphonso Lingis, *The Visible and the Invisible*, Evanston, Northwestern University Press, 1968.

Ortega y Gasset, José, 'Meditaciones del Quijote' Obras Completas, Madrid, Revista de Occidence, 1946–7, trans. E. Rugg and D. Marín, *Meditations on Quixote*, New York, W.W. Norton, 1963.

Index

An asterisk indicates the abbreviated title of a poem. For a list of these titles see pages 139–140.